A Few Minutes A Day

A Few Minutes A Day

by
Dicy Reaugh Hall

illustrated by
Brittany Virott

George Ronald, Publisher
46 High Street, Kidlington, Oxford OX5 2DN

© Dicy Reaugh Hall 2002
All Rights Reserved

A catalogue record for this book is available
from the British Library

ISBN 0-85398-452-2

Typesetting & Cover Design by Alexander Leith
www.yander.com

Printed and bound in Great Britain by Biddles Ltd
www.biddles.co.uk

Contents

	Preface	vii
	To the Teacher	ix
1.	The Month of Bahá: Splendour	1
2.	The Month of Jalál: Glory	15
3.	The Month of Jamál: Beauty	29
4.	The Month of 'Aẓamat: Grandeur	43
5.	The Month of Núr: Light	57
6.	The Month of Raḥmat: Mercy	77
7.	The Month of Kalimát: Words	91
8.	The Month of Kamál: Perfection	105
9.	The Month of Asmá': Names	119
10.	The Month of 'Izzat: Might	133
11.	The Month of Mashíyyat: Will	145
12.	The Month of 'Ilm: Knowledge	159
13.	The Month of Qudrat: Power	175
14.	The Month of Qawl: Speech	189
15.	The Month of Masá'il: Questions	205
16.	The Month of Sharaf: Honour	221
17.	The Month of Sulṭán: Sovereignty	237
18.	The Month of Mulk: Dominion	253
	Ayyám-i-Há: Intercalary Days	267
19.	The Month of 'Alá': Loftiness	271
	Bibliography	285
	Where the Readings Come From	287

For those who encourage us
we will take giant steps

Thank you dear Ray and Nance Meyer

Preface

This book is built around the idea that it is important for young Bahá'ís to learn something of the Bahá'í Faith every day, to read or recite something from the holy writings, to reflect on and consult about what has been learned and to put into practice the Bahá'í teachings. It is designed for primary school aged children but can be adapted for younger and older children as well.

The book provides the teacher or parent with simple tools with which to teach the child the importance of daily prayer and to give him or her an understanding of the Bahá'í teachings and the practice of consultation so that the child will develop good morals, a sense of self-worth and good patterns of behaviour. The lessons are planned around basic themes which can be expanded with the growth and needs of the child.

Using these themes, which are central to the ongoing cycles of Bahá'í life, the teacher can help set patterns of thought which will be useful to the child as he or she develops as an individual and which he or she can easily apply and draw on throughout life. A quotation from the Bahá'í writings has been chosen for each theme being studied but it should not be thought that the quotation is related to the day on which it appears or is in some way a definition of that day. As the teacher follows a theme, any other quotation which appears to be suitable may be chosen instead.

The lessons are kept very short, to a few minutes a day. This is an easily managed time frame for most people and enables the child and the teacher or parent to have quality time together that is not too burdensome or demanding.

It is hoped that these simple lessons will inspire and deeply motivate the child to learn and think. As the teacher in many instances will be a parent, just having this time together every day will be important for the child. Using the parent's or teacher's own interest in him or her as a reward, the child will particularly enjoy the consultation period as a time to communicate and reinforce what he or she learns to value.

This is not a comprehensive study of the Bahá'í Faith but rather a helping hand to challenge, inspire and begin the process of daily learning, which every Bahá'í knows is ongoing and ever-advancing. In the Four Valleys Bahá'u'lláh quotes from Rúmí's Mathnavi:

> The lover's teacher is the Loved One's beauty,
> His face their lesson and their only book.
> Learning of wonderment, of longing love their duty,
> Not on learned chapters and dull themes they look.
> The chain that binds them is His musky hair,
> The Cyclic Scheme to them, is but to Him a stair.

Thus our own enthrallment to God, to His Messengers and His covenant will be an example to our children which will enable them to set out on their own path towards God. Teaching and learning happen simultaneously and both these will begin to develop during these few minutes a day.

To the Teacher

This book is written for the child but it is hoped that you will work alongside the child day by day and go through the book with him or her. As the lessons are designed to take place every day, it is likely that you will be the child's parent and therefore you will both benefit from the close relationship that develops when people work together on a project. You will also be able to appreciate the level of your child's understanding and his or her ability to cope with a particular lesson. In turn, your child will grow to understand what you believe to be important and will develop respect and love.

The lessons for each day should be seen as starting points rather than as fixed or obligatory. The choice of activities, consultations and prayers is limitless and no doubt you will want to use some of the suggestions and not others. If the child has needs or the relationship between you raises concerns different from those considered in the lesson, these should be incorporated into the lesson. In my view, the important thing is to capture the child's interest. Some activities or themes may interest neither teacher nor student, so why not choose something else to do or to talk about?

Although this book is geared towards the primary school aged child, your pre-schooler should not be underestimated. His or her understanding may well exceed your expectations. In any case, it is always interesting for older people to observe that freedom of thought which such young children possess. If you are the child's grandparent using this book, you may recall what you thought you had forgotten. Indeed, the whole Bahá'í community may be surprised at the useful opinions expressed at a consultation by young children!

1

Month of Bahá
(Splendour)

A Prayer to Remember

Read this prayer. Try to memorize it by the end of the month. You will be able to do this if you learn a small part each day:

> I have wakened in Thy shelter, O my God, and it becometh him that seeketh that shelter to abide within the Sanctuary of Thy protection and the Stronghold of Thy defence. Illumine my inner being, O my Lord, with the splendours of the Dayspring of Thy Revelation, even as Thou didst illumine my outer being with the morning light of Thy favour.
>
> *Bahá'u'lláh*

Activity

The dictionary meaning of splendour is 'great light or lustre: brilliance'. For today's activity, first discuss this idea and then with paper and scissors make a star that looks very bright and brilliant! It could be coloured with a shiny crayon.

For Consultation

Tonight may be the time to share your star with your family or community. Explain the meaning of 'splendour' and ask family members what splendour means in a Bahá'í's life.

DAY 2

A Prayer to Remember

Concentrate on learning this part of the prayer.

I have wakened in Thy shelter, O my God …

Activity

Do you have a pen pal? Someone to whom you could write and share ideas? Think of one and today write a letter to this person or community. Ask your friend if he or she feels it is a 'splendid' idea to be pen pals!

For Consultation

This letter will take some consultation between you and your parent or teacher. Think of all the possibilities of having a pen pal. Then discuss them.

DAY 3

A Prayer to Remember

I have wakened in Thy shelter, O my God, and it becometh him that seeketh that shelter to abide within the Sanctuary of Thy protection and the Stronghold of Thy defence.

Concentrate on learning this part of the prayer.

Activity

On a special piece of paper write down as much of your prayer as you can remember.

For Consultation

Soon it will be time to celebrate Riḍván. What do you know about Riḍván? Please discuss and/or read about Riḍván.

DAY 4

A Prayer to Remember

I have wakened in Thy shelter, O my God, and it becometh him that seeketh that shelter to abide within the Sanctuary of Thy protection and the Stronghold of Thy defence.

Concentrate on learning this part of the prayer. Say the prayer and write down what you now know.

Activity

Why not be a star … a very 'splendorous' star? Act it out. Try to stand 'shiny', jump 'shiny', walk 'shiny', etc.

For Consultation

What behaviour would be 'shiny'? How would a group of people with 'shiny' behaviour appear? What would the result be?

A Prayer to Remember

I have wakened in Thy shelter, O my God, and it becometh him that seeketh that shelter to abide within the Sanctuary of Thy protection and the Stronghold of Thy defence. Illumine my inner being, O my Lord …

Activity

With tissue or crepe paper you could make some lovely flowers of different types. Later you could add some of the Hidden Words of Bahá'u'lláh written on little slips of paper and tucked into the flowers! Then at Riḍván maybe you would be allowed to give them out to your friends at one of the meetings or perhaps at another Feast during the year, or whatever else you can think of and are allowed to do.

For Consultation

Talk this idea over with your parent or teacher. Telephone the secretary of the Local Spiritual Assembly or the Feast and Holy Days Committee member who could advise you whether this idea would be welcome.

A Prayer to Remember

I have wakened in Thy shelter, O my God, and it becometh him that seeketh that shelter to abide within the Sanctuary of Thy protection and the Stronghold of Thy defence. Illumine my inner being, O my Lord, with the splendours of the Day-Spring of Thy Revelation …

Activity

With the tissue or crepe paper begin making the flowers. You may need a bit of time to learn how to fold them and turn them out. Perhaps you have a book that teaches this or a friend or teacher at school knows how. Make a few today.

For Consultation

Buddha was a Messenger of God who lived 2500 years ago. The story of how He became enlightened is beautiful. Buddha said,

> I am not the first Buddha who came upon this earth, nor shall I be the last. In due time another Buddha will arise in the world, a Holy One, a supremely enlightened One, endowed with wisdom in conduct, auspicious, knowing the universe, an incomparable leader of men, a Master of angels and mortals. He will reveal to you the same eternal truths which I have taught you. He will preach to you His religion, glorious in its origin, glorious at the climax and glorious at the goal, in the spirit and in the letter. He will proclaim a religious life, wholly perfect and pure, such as I now proclaim. His disciples will number many thousands, while Mine number many hundreds.

What do you think Buddha was referring to in this sermon?

DAY 7

A Prayer to Remember

> I have wakened in Thy shelter, O my God, and it becometh him that seeketh that shelter to abide within the Sanctuary of Thy protection and the Stronghold of Thy defence. Illumine my inner being, O my Lord, with the splendours of the Day-Spring of Thy Revelation …

Is your prayer becoming more familiar to you?

Activity
Make a few more paper flowers. Find some sturdy twigs to use for stems while you are outside today!

For Consultation
Buddha was called 'the Enlightened One'. What does this mean to you?

A Prayer to Remember
I have wakened in Thy shelter, O my God, and it becometh him that seeketh that shelter to abide within the Sanctuary of Thy protection and the Stronghold of Thy defence. Illumine my inner being, O my Lord, with the splendours of the Day-Spring of Thy Revelation …

Activity
Make more paper flowers and insert the stems. These can be stapled, tied, glued or taped to the underside of the paper. Place them in a large bowl or vase ready for the next step tomorrow.

For Consultation
Share a song today! If you know it, 'Shine Your Light on Me, Bahá'u'lláh' would be wonderful, for example.

A Prayer
Just for today you could read this prayer of 'Abdu'l-Bahá:

O God, my God! Increase Thou this fire, as day followeth day, till the blast of it setteth in motion all the earth. O Thou, my Lord! Kindle the light of Thy love in every heart, breathe into men's souls the spirit of Thy knowledge, gladden their breasts with the verses of Thy oneness. Call Thou to life those who dwell in their tombs, warn Thou the prideful, make happiness world-wide, send down Thy crystal waters, and in the assemblage of manifest splendours pass round that cup which is 'tempered at the camphor fountain'.

'Abdu'l-Bahá

Activity

You will now need the book *The Hidden Words of Bahá'u'lláh* to find the verses you will use for this activity. How many verses you choose all depends on how many flowers you have made. Write the verses down on the slips of paper, very clearly.

For Consultation

Bahá'u'lláh wrote *The Hidden Words* in 1858 as He walked along the banks of the Tigris River. These words are really the essence of religion. What would our behaviour be like if we lived by them? Aren't the words shining examples of what God wants from us? Consult about this.

DAY 10

A Prayer to Remember

I have wakened in Thy shelter, O my God, and it becometh him that seeketh that shelter to abide within the Sanctuary of Thy protection and the Stronghold of Thy defence. Illumine my inner being, O my Lord, with the splendours of the Day-Spring of Thy Revelation, even as Thou didst illumine my outer being with the morning light of Thy favour.

Repeat your prayer by heart. If you need help, ask your parent or teacher. Well done!

Activity

Today, fold the small slips of paper in half or whatever you like, very carefully, and insert them deeply into the folds of the middle of each flower. The idea is that you will then pass around the vase of flowers at the meeting which has been chosen for this and give one flower to each person present. Be sure you do this with love and respect for the friends so that they become very happy! When each person has a flower, the friends can reach into their flowers and find a Hidden Word which can then be read. Each can take his flower home as a memory of a beautiful meeting. Keep the flowers safe until you use them.

For Consultation

Ask the members of your family what their favourite Hidden Word is.

DAY 11

A Prayer Remembered

Recite a prayer that you know by heart. Can you say a different one for each remaining day of the month?

Activity

Perhaps your family has recent Bahá'í magazines or books which include photographs of the splendours of the Bahá'í Temples around the world, the Shrine of the Báb, the Shrine of Bahá'u'lláh, Bahjí, the Seat of the Universal

House of Justice, the other buildings on the Arc or the Terraces. See if you can collect photographs and put them out on the table.

For Consultation

Ask your parent or teacher to explain each of these photographs to you. What is significant about each building? Have any of your family or friends been there? Can they tell you more about them? Would you like to visit there?

DAY 12

A Prayer Remembered

Recite another prayer that you know by heart.

Activity

Congratulations on the beautiful flowers you have completed! Today give your parents or teacher a treat and tell them a make-believe story about the flowers ... just use your hopes and dreams and maybe what you learned from *The Hidden Words*!

For Consultation

One of the Hidden Words tells us that God created us all out of the same dust. Can you find the Hidden Word? Can you talk about what you feel is meant by this?

DAY 13

Prayer to Remember

I have wakened in Thy shelter, O my God, and it becometh him that seeketh that shelter to abide within the Sanctuary of Thy protection and the Stronghold of Thy defence. Illumine my inner being, O my Lord, with the splendours of the Day-Spring of Thy Revelation, even as Thou didst illumine my outer being with the morning light of Thy favour.

If you have managed to learn this prayer by heart, you must be very pleased about it. Now you will always have it in your heart – did you know that? Please repeat your prayer as usual.

Activity

When we speak of the essence of religion, we can compare all religions. What do all the major religions of the world have in common? Make a list of some of these principles, the ones you feel all religions agree on.

For Consultation

Some principles were given to humankind for this day by Bahá'u'lláh. Discuss these and perhaps in your free time today you can look these up in a Bahá'í book so that you know them.

DAY 14

A Prayer Remembered

Recite another prayer that you know by heart, if possible.

Activity

Add the list of Bahá'í principles to the list you made yesterday of what all the religions agree on and compare these.

For Consultation

What does your parent or teacher think of your list? Why?

DAY 15

A Prayer Remembered

Recite another prayer that you know by heart.

Activity

Activity time today will be your choice! You might make a dessert or bread or something else your family can eat or drink. Of perhaps you could make some play dough for another day's activity. If you make the play dough (keep it airtight) you might like to make extra for friends and plan a nice surprise for them!

There are two kinds of play dough. One is soft and squishy and can be kept a long time if you keep it in a sealed container. The other is for modelling and can be dried and then painted. Here are the recipes.

For squishy play dough
2½ cups flour
2 cups boiling water
½ cup salt
2–3 tablespoons oil
1 tablespoon food colouring

Directions:
Combine dry ingredients. Stir in the boiling water and oil. Divide into parts and add different food colours to each. Store in an airtight container in the refrigerator.

For hard-drying play dough
4 cups flour
1½ cups warm water
1 cup salt
Food colouring, if desired

Directions:
Mix dry ingredients, add water. Knead 7 to 10 minutes until smooth and elastic. Add food colouring. Make desired items and allow to air dry. Items can then be painted.

For Consultation

If you elect to make food or drink, consult on a special way to serve it to your family tonight and plan it!

DAY 16

A Prayer Remembered

Recite another prayer that you know by heart. Can you still remember the prayer you learned this month? Good!

Activity

This month is nearly over and Feast will be here shortly. Make a little container for your personal fund box today. I expect you can think what will come next!

For Consultation

Giving to the Bahá'í fund is a privilege. Two things now. Consult on why Bahá'ís wish to give to their fund and why it is a privilege. If you truly understand this and feel you would like (or love) to give to the fund, talk together about the ways you could earn money that would be yours to give.

A Prayer Remembered

Recite another prayer that you know by heart. Before you say your prayer, think about the words and be sure you continue to think about what the prayer means.

Activity

Play dough! It is great to make things and experiment with them. With your play dough make something that makes you think of the word 'splendour' (e.g. a star, sun, Bahá'í building, fund box, etc.). If you didn't make play dough or don't have any clay or mud, try drawing it.

For Consultation

You may have already earned something to put into your personal fund box or container. How did it feel when you made that contribution? What do you want to happen by giving your contribution?

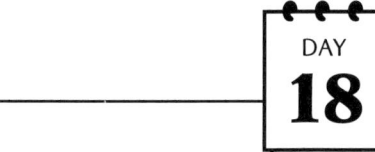

A Prayer Remembered

Recite another prayer that you know by heart.

Activity

If you have received a letter back from your pen pal, you could now answer it! Or you could draw for your friend a picture of something you have learned this month. Alternatively, you could begin a diary to keep for yourself or to share with friends.

For Consultation

Here are two questions for you: How long has God existed? How long will God exist? Ask other members of your family what they think.

A Prayer Remembered

Recite another prayer that you know by heart.

Activity

Do you know what an 'illuminated prayer' is? It is a written prayer with designs or pictures drawn around it to make it look beautiful. Try making a simple illuminated prayer. As neatly as possible, in any style of writing you like, write out the prayer you have learned this month. Then, around the outside edges draw a design or picture and colour it in. Take your time. You might like to cover it with clear plastic or contact paper. It would make a nice gift or a precious keepsake of the work you did this month!

For Consultation

Thinking back through this month, or looking back through the pages, what would you say about the meaning of the month of Bahá (Splendour)?

2

Month of Jalál
(Glory)

DAY 1

A Prayer to Remember

Glory be to Thee, O God, for Thy manifestation of love to mankind! O Thou Who art our Life and Light, guide Thy servants in Thy way, and make us rich in Thee and free from all save Thee.

Bahá'u'lláh

Activity

'Bahá'u'lláh' means 'the Glory of God' in Arabic. Bahá'u'lláh was born into a wealthy family descended from ancient Persian kings. Bahá'u'lláh lived from 1817 to 1892 and experienced imprisonment, torture and exile from Persia to Baghdad, Constantinople, Adrianople and 'Akká in the Holy Land. He is buried at Bahjí, near 'Akká, and this is the Point of Adoration towards which Bahá'ís turn when we say our obligatory prayers.

Get a compass and work out which way to face when praying.

For Consultation

Why might we be asked to pray in a certain position or direction?

DAY 2

A Prayer to Remember

Learn this portion of the prayer by heart. You'll be able to recite it all by the end of this Bahá'í month.

> Glory be to Thee, O God, for Thy manifestation of love to mankind!

Activity

Yesterday we learned that Bahá'u'lláh was born in Persia, now called Iran, in 1817. Find Iran on a map. Locate the country where you live. Is it a long way from Iran?

For Consultation

Bahá'u'lláh said, 'The earth is but one country, and mankind its citizens.' What does this mean?

A Prayer to Remember

Glory be to Thee, O God, for Thy manifestation of love to mankind!

Activity

One dictionary definition of glory is 'adoration, thanksgiving and praise offered in worship'. Paint a watercolour picture or fingerpaint a scene in which people are praying. Think of different ways people might look when they pray.

For Consultation

Here is a question for you and you can also ask members of your family for their opinion: What is a prayer?

DAY 4

A Prayer to Remember

> Glory be to Thee, O God, for Thy manifestation of love to mankind! O Thou Who art our Life and Light …

Write down the part of the prayer you can remember.

Activity

Here is a reading from Bahá'u'lláh on the subject of prayer. Read it and then draw it as you picture it in your mind:

> Whoso reciteth, in the privacy of his chamber, the verses revealed by God, the scattering angels of the Almighty shall scatter abroad the fragrance of the words uttered by his mouth, and shall cause the heart of every righteous man to throb. Though he may, at first, remain unaware of its effect, yet the virtue of the grace vouchsafed unto him must needs sooner or later exercise its influence upon his soul.
>
> *Bahá'u'lláh*

For Consultation

Talk with your parent or teacher about the reading and explain your drawing.

DAY 5

A Prayer to Remember

> Glory be to Thee, O God, for Thy manifestation of love to mankind! O Thou Who art our Life and Light …

Activity

Make a pretend instrument, or instruments, and one for your teacher as well. Try to compose some glorious music, using such instruments as the lids of saucepans, spoons, kitchen implements, blocks, chimes, etc. Enjoy trying to work out a harmony!

We have prayers set to music, can you sing one? (e.g. Blessed is the Spot)

DAY 6

A Prayer to Remember

Glory be to Thee, O God, for Thy manifestation of love to mankind! O Thou Who art our Life and Light, guide Thy servants in Thy way ...

Activity

Make a list of the Bahá'í Holy Days on which work and school should be suspended. Hint: There are nine of these.

For Consultation

Do you or your family go to work or school on these days? What do you think about it?

DAY 7

A Prayer to Remember

Glory be to Thee, O God, for Thy manifestation of love to mankind! O Thou Who art our Life and Light, guide Thy servants in Thy way …

Activity

Do some role playing of activities at your house on a Holy Day. Maybe you could show the different ways people prepare for a Holy Day or people saying prayers or dressing nicely. It doesn't have to be what you actually do but how you would like it or imagine it to be.

For Consultation

What will it be like when the whole world knows about Bahá'u'lláh? Wonder about it!

DAY 8

A Prayer to Remember

Glory be to Thee, O God, for Thy manifestation of love to mankind! O Thou Who art our Life and Light, guide Thy servants in Thy way, and make us rich in Thee and free from all save Thee.

Bahá'u'lláh

Say your prayer without looking and if you need help, ask for it.

Activity

Get out your play dough and shape a Spiritual Assembly. A Spiritual Assembly is nine of the Bahá'ís in your community who are elected to oversee, or administer, the affairs of the Bahá'ís who reside there. Move the nine shapes around so that they can consult, as Spiritual Assembly members do at a meeting.

For Consultation

Talk about your Spiritual Assembly. If you don't have one in your area, write to one nearby and ask them about what they do.

A Prayer to Remember

Say your prayer by heart. See Day 8 for the whole prayer if you need help.

Activity

Ask your parent or teacher to help you find a Bahá'í history book – or borrow one – and begin a more detailed study of the life of Bahá'u'lláh. We are going to make a time line to show the different parts of His life.

For Consultation

What is a time line? Consult about what needs to be on it.

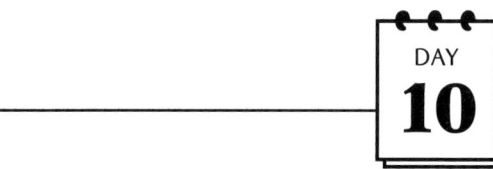

A Prayer to Remember

Say your prayer by heart. If your prayer is memorized, be sure and share it with your family and friends.

Activity

Read about the life of Bahá'u'lláh. On a sheet of paper, write in the important dates in His life. You can keep this with your map and clip it together as your very own reference file. When you get older it will be so handy!

For Consultation
Talk about the time line with the members of your family tonight.

A Prayer to Remember
For today read this prayer for service to God:
> Let my food, O my Lord, be Thy beauty, and my drink the light of Thy presence, and my hope Thy pleasure, and my work Thy praise …
>
> *Bahá'u'lláh*

Activity
Tell your parent or teacher a story about your favourite animal friend. Explain what the animal's life was like and how you took care of it.

For Consultation
Should we be kind to animals?

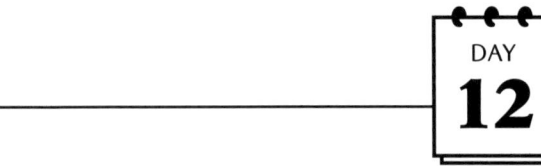

A Prayer to Remember
Say the prayer you have memorized for this month. Do you still remember last month's prayer?

Activity
Make your parent or teacher a cup of tea or coffee or whatever they prefer and prepare for consultation.

For Consultation

Should we learn to take care of others before we take care of ourselves?

A Prayer to Remember

Say your prayer for this month by heart.

Activity

Draw a picture of the sun shining on the major religions of the world: the Bahá'í Faith, the Bábí religion, Islam, Christianity, Zoroastrianism, Judaism, Hinduism, Buddhism and Sabeanism. Do not draw the Prophets of God – draw the people they taught. It is not respectful to draw a Manifestation of God.

For Consultation

Discuss the lessons we have learned from the various Messengers of God: Krishna – renunciation of the world; Moses – law; Zoroaster – good over evil; Buddha – enlightenment; Christ – love; Muḥammad – nation-building; the Báb – Herald of Bahá'u'lláh; Bahá'u'lláh – unity of humankind. (These examples are a guide only.)

DAY 14

A Prayer to Remember
Say your prayer for this month by heart.

Activity
Find some leftover fabric and glue it to the edges of the picture you drew yesterday. You could keep it or give it to a friend.

For Consultation
Why does God send so many teachers to the world with new messages?

DAY 15

A Prayer to Remember
Say your prayer for this month by heart.

Activity
It's time to dance! Put on some music you like and try to do a fun dance. You could tell a story with your hands like a hula or you could imitate animals or do different walks.

For Consultation

What do you know about the Son of God, Jesus Christ? What do Christians believe?

DAY 16

A Story

Instead of your prayer today, read this story about Jesus Christ as told by 'Abdu'l-Bahá, the son of Bahá'u'lláh:

> Jesus was a poor man. One night when He was out in the fields, the rain began to fall. He had no place to go for shelter so He lifted His eyes toward heaven saying, 'O Father! For the birds of the air Thou hast created nests, for the sheep a fold, for the animals dens, for the fish places of refuge, but for Me Thou hast provided no shelter. There is no place where I may lay My head. My bed consists of the cold ground; My lamps at night are the stars and My food is the grass of the field. Yet who upon earth is richer than I? For the greatest blessing Thou hast not given to the rich and mighty but unto Me, for Thou hast given Me the poor. To Me Thou hast granted this blessing. They are Mine. Therefore am I the richest man on earth.'
>
> *'Abdu'l-Bahá*

Activity

Cut out pictures from old magazines of all the animals mentioned in this reading and glue them into a collage. Draw their beds and shelters.

For Consultation

Is there a story from the New Testament (the holy book of Christianity) that you could share and discuss? Or read any passage from the Bible and discuss it.

DAY 17

A Prayer to Remember
Say your prayer for this month by heart.

Activity
The Feast of Jamál is in three days' time! Find a recipe that you could prepare for the Feast. Decide what ingredients you might need from the shop and give your parent or teacher a list.

For Consultation
How is your fund container? Is it being used regularly or as often as you would like? You could consult about this.

DAY 18

A Prayer to Remember
Say your prayer for this month with love in your heart!

Activity
Write in your diary. You can include items you will later write to your pen pal about or you can keep track of ideas that you would like to discuss with your Bahá'í community or family.

For Consultation
'Character' is a combination of traits or qualities unique to each of us. What is your character like? Does your parent or teacher see you as you see yourself? Think about how this works.

DAY 19

A Prayer to Remember

Here is the prayer you memorized this month.

> Glory be to Thee, O God, for Thy manifestation of love to mankind!
> O Thou Who art our Life and Light, guide Thy servants in Thy way,
> and make us rich in Thee and free from all save Thee.
>
> *Bahá'u'lláh*

Congratulations on learning it so well.

Activity

Today you will need time to prepare the recipe you chose to make for the Nineteen Day Feast. Enjoy this and present it in a pleasant way!

For Consultation

Now is the time to review what you learned in the Bahá'í month of Jalál (Glory). What did you enjoy the most?

3

Month of Jamál
(Beauty)

A Reading to Remember

O thou sapling which hast grown in the garden of the love of God! Unloose thy tongue in thanksgiving to the kingdom of glory for having received the light of divine guidance while still a child and for being singled out, through His supreme bounty, as a choice plant in the Abhá Paradise. It is my hope that thou wilt become a child of the kingdom, wilt study arts, sciences and divine knowledge, mayest turn into a fruitful and flourishing tree in the Vineyard of God and that, through the sprinkling of the clouds of His living providence, thou mayest appear in the utmost freshness and tender beauty.
And upon thee be salutation and praise.

'Abdu'l-Bahá

Activity

This prayer is from 'Abdu'l-Bahá, who was the son of Bahá'u'lláh. He lived a life so devout and in such service to His father that He is known as the Mystery of God. Many people keep a photograph of Him where they can see it often because He is an example to Bahá'ís and a source of great love and motivation. Ask for a photograph of Him to keep in your prayer book or in a picture frame.

For Consultation

This reading is full of words which may need to be explained. They are used symbolically – that is, one word stands for something else – which brings great beauty to them. Look up in a dictionary whatever words are difficult to understand or ask your parents or teacher to explain them to you.

DAY 2

Reading

Here is a story about 'Abdu'l-Bahá. As you read, write down or ask your parent or teacher to note what you find moving, interesting or of historical importance. This story is from a book by Myron Phelps, an American lawyer who was a guest of 'Abdu'l-Bahá for one month in 1902.

> Some day at this season ... you may see the poor of 'Akká gathered at one of the shops where clothes are sold, receiving cloaks from the Master. Upon many, especially the most infirm or crippled, he himself places the garment, adjusts it with his own hands, and strokes it approvingly, as if to say, 'There! Now you will do well.' ...
> On feast days he visits the poor at their homes. He chats with them, inquires into their health and comfort, mentions by name those who are absent, and leaves gifts for all.
> ... He himself eats but once a day, and then bread, olives, and cheese suffice him.
> His room is small and bare, with only a matting on the stone floor. His habit is to sleep upon this floor. Not long ago a friend, thinking that this must be hard for a man of advancing years, presented him with a bed fitted with springs and mattress. So these stand in his room also, but are rarely used. 'For how', he says, 'can

I bear to sleep in luxury when so many of the poor have not even shelter?' So he lies upon the floor and covers himself only with his cloak.

… He is the beloved of all the city, high and low. And how could it be otherwise? For to this man it is the law, as it was to Jesus of Nazareth, to do good to those who injure him.

… The Master is as simple as his soul is great. He claims nothing for himself – neither comfort, nor honour, nor repose. Three or four hours of sleep suffice him; all the remainder of his time and all his strength are given to the succour of those who suffer, in spirit or in body. 'I am', he says, 'the servant of God.'

Such is 'Abbás Effendi, the Master of 'Akká.

DAY 3

A Reading to Remember

Read the words of 'Abdu'l-Bahá that you read on the first day of this month. This is a long verse and will be a challenge to memorize but do try! Reading it every day will help you to learn it by heart.

Activity

Now might be a great time to become familiar with the Bahá'í calendar. Bahá'í days start at sunset and run until sunset the next day. Copy out the Bahá'í calendar for this month of Jamál (Beauty). Fill in school days, special events and Bahá'í meetings. Get to know this calendar and the Bahá'í anniversaries.

For Consultation

The Báb devised the Bahá'í calendar and Bahá'u'lláh approved it. What else do you know about the Báb? What does His name mean? Why is He called 'the Gate'?

A Reading to Remember

Read the words of 'Abdu'l-Bahá that you read on the first day of this month.

Activity

Poems can be fun to write. Write or dictate a poem about this month's subject, 'beauty'.

For Consultation

Share your poem and say how you feel about it.

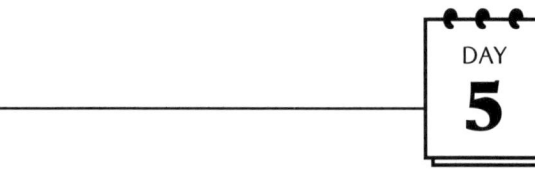

A Reading to Remember

Read the words of 'Abdu'l-Bahá that you read on the first day of this month.

Activity

Take a look at your poem again. Would you like to present it to your Bahá'í friends at the next Feast or meeting? Learn it by heart and make any changes you like. Practise it often before the time you present it to the community.

For Consultation

Consult on the question: What is the most wonderful thing in the world? Probably many different answers will come to light.

DAY 6

A Reading to Remember

Read the words of 'Abdu'l-Bahá that you read on the first day of this month.

Activity

You are probably beginning to compile a small mound of work which has been generated by all of these activities! Perhaps the idea of 'publishing' your own book appeals to you. By tying the pages neatly together or putting them into a binder, you will have a workbook that you can add to as you learn new things. Design a cover today.

For Consultation

Talk about beauty. What would life be like without it? Does everyone see beauty?

DAY 7

A Reading to Remember

Read the words of 'Abdu'l-Bahá that you read on the first day of this month.

Activity

Find some pretty leaves or pieces of plants to paste onto a page in your book. Chose ones that you find BEAUTIFUL.

For Consultation

What do you think is beautiful about all religions? Ask your family what they feel is beautiful about the future of religion as well as religion in the past and today.

DAY 8

A Reading to Remember

Read the words of 'Abdu'l-Bahá that you read on the first day of this month.

Activity

Wait until tonight to do this day's activity. Ask all of your family to go outside together where there is a clear view of the sky and look up at the stars. If you have a book on astronomy, see which stars and constellations can be found in the part of the sky you see.

For Consultation

Bahá'u'lláh says: 'Great is thy blessedness, O earth, for thou hast been made the foot-stool of thy God, and been chosen as the seat of His mighty throne.' Take a torch outside with you tonight and discuss this quotation under the sky!

A Reading to Remember

Read the words of 'Abdu'l-Bahá that you read on the first day of this month. How is your memorization coming along?

Activity

Write out your prayer and illuminate it.

Reflection

Here is a question to think about today and to hear what your parents or teacher think and say about it: What do we learn when we have problems in our lives? Think of some examples.

A Reading to Remember

Say as much of your reading as you know and ask for help. Look at the first day of the month for the whole passage.

Activity

Look at your Bahá'í calendar and tell your teacher today's date.

For Consultation

The dictionary says that beauty is 'a part, characteristic or attribute that arouses delight; a specific excellence or grace'. How is beauty a part of our life?

DAY 11

A Reading to Remember
Try to say the whole verse by heart – keep going!

Activity
Sing some beautiful songs that you know or sing a prayer, making up your own tune.

For Consultation
You may have been to one or more of the Bahá'í Temples. Even if you have not, you can look at pictures of them. You will probably agree that they are quite beautiful. Why are they beautiful?

DAY 12

A Reading to Remember
Read the words of 'Abdu'l-Bahá that you read on the first day of this month.

Activity
Write in your diary to catch up with what you have been doing. Do you enjoy it? If you have a camera, perhaps a friend could take a photo of you and your parents or teacher. Or you could draw a picture of yourself with your parents or teacher.

For Consultation

Are your parents and teacher important to you? Did you know that Bahá'u'lláh said that any teacher, before teaching another person, should teach himself first? This is so that the words of the teacher will attract the hearts of those who hear him.

A Reading to Remember

With great feeling, read the words of 'Abdu'l-Bahá that you read on the first day of this month.

Activity

Use your play dough or pen to design a beautiful school. What would be included in a room? Would there even be a room? Would there be a beautiful shape to the room or furniture? Use your imagination.

For Consultation

In the future when little children go to school, what should they study? Write down your answer and present it to your Bahá'í community during the consultation time at Feast if you feel it would be of value to others.

A Reading to Remember

Read the words of 'Abdu'l-Bahá that you read on the first day of this month.

Activity

Do you know any funny jokes? Share a joke or two and have a good laugh!

For Consultation

Share and talk about this reading:

> This is the Day whereon the Ocean of God's mercy hath been manifested unto men, the Day in which the Day Star of His loving-kindness hath shed its radiance upon them, the Day in which the clouds of His bountiful favour have overshadowed the whole of mankind. Now is the time to cheer and refresh the down-cast through the invigorating breeze of love and fellowship, and the living waters of friendliness and charity.
>
> *Bahá'u'lláh*

A Reading to Remember

Can you say the entire passage you have been reading? If so, this is wonderful! If not, please keep trying.

Activity

Do you have the time and ability to take a walk today? If so, please do and make it very special. Take notice of things that are beautiful.

For Consultation

Can you find beauty even in a place that does not appear beautiful?

A Reading to Remember

Please say the whole verse you have been learning.

Activity

Meditate for a few minutes on this past month of beauty. When we meditate we listen to what is inside of us, very quietly.

For Consultation

What was it like to meditate?

DAY 17

A Reading to Remember

Please say the whole verse you have been learning.

Activity

Draw a beautiful picture to add to your book.

For Consultation

Do you have any questions which you would like to ask your parents or teacher? Think and ask.

DAY 18

A Reading to Remember

Please say the whole verse you have been learning.

Activity

Draw a beautiful picture to give to your teacher at school.

For Consultation

Talk about and act out how to give someone a precious gift. What is a precious gift?

A Reading to Remember

Please say the whole verse you have been learning. You have done well!

Activity

Check your hands and fingernails. Do you like them nice and clean? Do your nails need cutting? You might like to clean them now. Be beautiful! 'Abdu'l-Bahá said,

> A child that is cleanly, agreeable, of good character, well-behaved – even though he be ignorant – is preferable to a child that is rude, unwashed, ill-natured, and yet becoming deeply versed in all the sciences and arts.

4

Month of 'Aẓamat (Grandeur)

A Reading to Remember

Instead of a prayer this month, here is a Hidden Word you can memorize:

> O Son of Man! My majesty is My gift to thee, and My grandeur the token of My mercy unto thee.
>
> *Bahá'u'lláh*

Activity

The dictionary describes grandeur as 'greatness and splendour'. Take some building blocks and build something that makes you think of greatness and splendour or 'grandeur'.

For Consultation

Discuss the Hidden Word above. What does it mean?

DAY 2

A Reading to Remember

Repeat yesterday's Hidden Word.

Activity

Cut out some pieces of thick paper or construction paper. Staple or fix these pieces together so that they stand upright and support each other. You could also use small sticks or whatever is available.

For Consultation

Shoghi Effendi, the Guardian of the Bahá'í Faith and the grandson of 'Abdu'l-Bahá, oversaw the construction of many Bahá'í buildings and holy places. He also developed much of the administrative order of the Bahá'í Faith. The buildings and the administration of the Bahá'í community are very much examples of grandeur. Shoghi Effendi made it easier for the Bahá'ís to understand the greatness of God and the Revelation of Bahá'u'lláh and His law. Discuss this.

DAY 3

A Reading to Remember

Read the Hidden Word you read on the first day.

A Reading

Here is a story about Shoghi Effendi from the book *The Crown of Beauty*. When you hear this story you can think of the GRANDEUR which Shoghi Effendi gave to the world through his great service to the Faith:

> Shoghi Effendi had grown up in the home of 'Abdu'l-Bahá. He had been shaped and guided by him and the love they bore for each other was deep and abiding. And yet, outside this bond, Shoghi Effendi had demonstrated from earliest childhood a devotion to the Faith of Bahá'u'lláh that was beyond his close filial attachment to his beloved grandfather. Proficient in several languages, he had served 'Abdu'l-Bahá as secretary and interpreter for some years. Even now he was attending Oxford University in order to perfect himself in English, as was 'Abdu'l-Bahá's wish.
>
> The new young Guardian returned to the Holy Land to shoulder the enormous task of guiding the community of Bahá'ís, now scattered about the five continents, into the world religion it was destined to become. Soon the Bahá'ís were abundantly aware of the priceless gift bestowed upon them. Shoghi Effendi was their Guardian, the appointed leader of their Faith – but he was also a

comrade in service, their 'true brother', as he signed his letter to them …

It devolved upon Shoghi Effendi to transmit the dream and prophecy into visible reality. He was the 'master designer', the one who could envision the end from the beginning. It was he who raised the superstructure of the Shrine of the Báb; who built the classical Greek-styled Archives Building nestled into the side of the mountain; who chose the site for the majestic headquarters of the Universal House of Justice. Just below on the rising slope he created a memorial garden of tranquil beauty as the final resting-place for members of 'Abdu'l-Bahá's family.

For Consultation

What have you just learned about Shoghi Effendi?

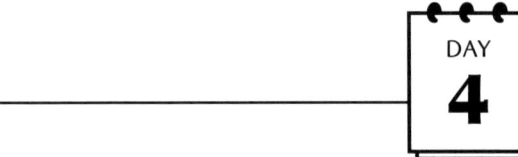

DAY 4

A Reading to Remember

Repeat the Hidden Word you read on the first day.

Activity

Write to your pen pal again or to another friend. Do you have any friends who speak a different language? Write down a few words you would like to know in that language.

For Consultation

Why are there so many languages in the world? Bahá'u'lláh said we should have one universal auxiliary language. What does that mean?

DAY 5

A Reading to Remember

Repeat the Hidden Word, then write down as much of it as you can remember.

Activity

Bahá'í law is very important to Bahá'ís. This is how they remain obedient to the covenant (or contract) which guides us. A Bahá'í must first recognize Bahá'u'lláh and then be obedient to His laws. Take a sheet of paper and label it 'Bahá'í Laws'. As we come across these laws you can note them down. One law is that Bahá'ís are to say an obligatory prayer every 24 hours. Add any other laws you already know.

For Consultation

How and when can a person become a Bahá'í and therefore need to observe Bahá'í laws?

DAY 6

A Reading to Remember

Read the Hidden Word you read on the first day.

Activity

The Tongue of Grandeur hath … in the Day of His Manifestation proclaimed: 'It is not his to boast who loveth his country, but it is his who loveth the world.'

Bahá'u'lláh

Write out this quotation and illuminate it.

For Consultation

How can we love the world?

A Prayer Remembered

Repeat a prayer you have learned by heart.

Activity

Another law to record is that from the age of maturity (15 years) a Bahá'í fasts for 19 days from sunrise to sunset during the month of 'Alá' (2–20 March). This is subject to certain conditions which Bahá'u'lláh has given us.

For Consultation

Describe the Bahá'í fast as if you were telling someone who didn't know about it. Is it a happy time?

A Reading to Remember

Say the Hidden Word we learned this month.

Activity

Another Bahá'í law states that in a town or city where there are at least nine Bahá'ís, a Spiritual Assembly should be formed. Include this on your list.

For Consultation

Bahá'u'lláh's book of law, the Kitáb-i-Aqdas, is the Most Holy Book. Why do you think this is?

DAY 9

A Reading to Remember

Say the Hidden Word we learned this month.

Activity

If your family or community has a copy of the Kitáb-i-Aqdas, look through it with your teacher.

For Consultation

Ask your teacher to explain some of the passages in the book to you and consult about these.

DAY 10

A Reading

From the Kitáb-i-Aqdas:

> Think not that We have revealed unto you a mere code of laws. Nay, rather, We have unsealed the choice Wine with the fingers of might and power. To this beareth witness that which the Pen of Revelation hath revealed. Meditate upon this, O men of insight!
>
> *Bahá'u'lláh*

Activity

Meditate on what you have learned about the laws of the Bahá'í Faith.

For Consultation

What do you know about the Báb? We will talk about this tomorrow.

DAY 11

A Prayer

Read a prayer from your prayer book.

Activity

Let's learn about Siyyid 'Alí-Muḥammad, who is called the Báb. On the eve of 23 May 1844 the Báb declared His mission to Mullá Ḥusayn, who was the first to believe in Him. The Báb called everyone to a 'new day', which some people had begun to feel was coming soon. Some were guided to the Báb and began to follow His teachings. He taught them that 'the Promised One' would soon appear with a great revelation and laws for a universal civilization and the Báb said that they should look for Him. The Báb was referring to

Bahá'u'lláh. The Báb was the Herald of Bahá'u'lláh, and although He brought an independent religion of His own, He called the people to search for the one who would bring the new day. Think about what this has meant to humankind.

Have you heard of John the Baptist? He told people about the coming of Jesus Christ. He told the people: 'Repent ye: for the kingdom of heaven is at hand' (Matthew 3:2). Jesus soon met with John and was baptized by him. This is when Jesus saw the Spirit of God descending onto Him like a dove. It is interesting to compare this with the fact that the Báb prepared the way for Bahá'u'lláh.

A Prayer Remembered

Please say any prayer you have learned.

Activity

Play act telling your friend about being a Bahá'í. What do you say to him or her? How do you tell him about it? Do you remember how to give someone a precious gift?

For Consultation

What is the best way to teach the Faith? (By example)

A Prayer to Remember

Say this prayer by the Báb.

> Is there any Remover of difficulties save God? Say: Praised be God! He is God! All are His servants, and all abide by His bidding!

Activity

Plan a fireside. Choose a theme or subject and perhaps a guest speaker. Decide what hospitality you are going to provide, for instance light refreshments, and think of the part friendship plays in the fireside.

For Consultation

When can you hold this fireside?

A Prayer Remembered

Say your favourite prayer!

Activity

Check your fund box. Is it heavier? Is it still interesting? Do you need to remodel it? Is there still plenty of room for more contributions? When will it be donated to the Bahá'í fund? Do you need more jobs to do so that you can continue to fill it up?

For Consultation

Talk about the meaning of SACRIFICE.

A Prayer

Find any prayer that reminds you of grandeur and say it.

Activity

Invite a friend to play today. Blow up some balloons together. If it's warm, fill them with water and play outdoors.

For Consultation

A friend is described in the dictionary as 'a person whom one knows, likes and trusts'. Consult on friendship. Think about the friends you have and why you call them 'friend'.

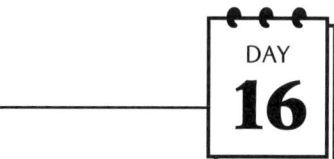

DAY 16

A Reading to Remember

Say your Hidden Word for this month.

Activity

Have a drink of lemonade or tea with your teacher and just talk because you are friends.

For Consultation
How do we take care of our bodies? Why does Bahá'u'lláh ask us to be clean, not to drink alcohol or take drugs? Why do we care for our bodies?

DAY 17

A Prayer Remembered
Say a prayer you know by heart.

Activity
Do you have a brother or sister? A young neighbour? Make today a special day for them by doing caring things for them, playing with them, reading them a story and finding ways to make them happy. Tell them about friendship.

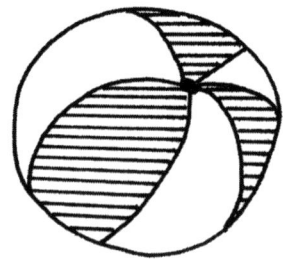

For Consultation
It is nearly time for the Nineteen Day Feast of Núr (Light). What have we learned about grandeur?

A Prayer

Say a prayer from your prayer book.

Activity

Find the clothes you will wear to the Feast and be sure they are ready. Can you iron? If you are allowed, press your clothes. Can you shine your shoes? Polish and shine them. You will look GRAND.

For Consultation

Why shouldn't we worry about things? What can we do to avoid worrying?

A Reading to Remember

Say the Hidden Word you have learned this month or any Hidden Word you know.

Activity

Tidy up your bookshelves and keep your Bahá'í books very neat. Make a bookmark with some material glued on strong paper.

For Consultation

We should read the Bahá'í writings every day. Why is this?

5

Month of Núr
(Light)

A Prayer to Remember

Learn this prayer by 'Abdu'l-Bahá by memorizing a line each day.

> O Thou compassionate Lord! O Lord of Hosts! Praise be unto Thee that Thou hast preferred these young children over the full grown and the matured, hast endowed them with Thy special bounty, hast guided them, hast bestowed upon them Thy Light and hast given them spirituality. Confirm us so that when we attain maturity we may be enabled to serve Thy kingdom, may train the souls, may become ignited candles and may shine like unto stars.
> Thou art the Giver, the Bestower and the Kind.
>
> *'Abdu'l-Bahá*

Activity

Turn on a light – a lamp – open the fridge – use a torch – whatever you like.

Think about the difference between having the light on and having it off. Discuss these observations – really look and really think.

For Consultation

The above prayer says that God has 'bestowed upon them Thy Light' and that it is hoped that the children will 'become ignited candles and may shine like unto stars'. What is this 'Light'?

DAY 2

A Prayer to Remember

Read 'Abdu'l-Bahá's very beautiful prayer again today and think about the words carefully.

Activity

You've experienced light that turns on and off. Now consider light that is constant. Draw an imaginary design of a light such as this. What is its fuel or what makes it run?

For Consultation

As an electrician connects wiring to an electric supply to create lighting in our homes, we also receive light from a channel ourselves. What is the source of the light and what is the channel? At dinner together discuss this with your family. Does this light ever stop?

DAY 3

A Prayer to Remember

Read 'Abdu'l-Bahá's beautiful prayer again. Tomorrow you will start to memorize it.

Activity

Look for three words in your prayer as you read it: 'light', 'ignited' and 'shine'. Draw the picture that comes to your mind when you say this prayer.

For Consultation

Could light and spirit be the same thing? What would they be 'made of'?

DAY 4

A Prayer to Remember

Begin to memorize your prayer by learning this portion:

> O Thou compassionate Lord! O Lord of Hosts!

Activity

Shine a light (i.e. torch) on your teacher or parent briefly and ask how he or she feels. Ask your teacher to shine a light on you. What can a light make you feel?

For Consultation

How can you share the feeling of light with someone else? How do you describe it — by words, deeds or feelings?

DAY 5

A Prayer to Remember

Learn this portion of the prayer by heart:

> O Thou compassionate Lord! O Lord of Hosts! Praise be unto Thee that Thou hast preferred these young children …

Activity

Today there is time to relax with a story …

Ios, the Shepherd Boy

These stories were told by 'Abdu'l-Bahá to Lua Getsinger, a beautiful and famous early American Bahá'í. 'Abdu'l-Bahá told her the stories to help her understand how someone who really loves God should behave and feel.

Ios Meets the King

Ios was a shepherd boy who looked after his flocks in the valleys and on the sloping hills of Persia. He was poor and simple and the only life he had ever known was looking after his sheep. There was only one thing he wanted in his life – he had a great longing to look on the face of his King. He had heard wonderful stories about his greatness and goodness, and Ios was sure that if he could only once behold the King's face he would live content and die happy.

One day Ios heard that the King and all his retinue would pass by on the highroad not far from where his sheep were grazing. Overcome by his good fortune and shaking with the intensity of his love for the King, Ios left everything and went to wait on the roadside. At last the Royal Procession appeared – musicians on horseback, soldiers and buglers glittering and splendid in their uniforms, banners flying bravely in the breeze, courtiers in magnificent clothes of silk, gold and silver, their jewels sparkling in the sunshine, and finally, bearing the object of all his longing, the Royal Carriage of the King.

Ios gazed on the approaching throng, his eyes searching for the King. With flushed face and throbbing heart, he watched for the face he had waited and longed for all his life.

Seeing that the procession had stopped, the King sent an aide to find the reason and was informed that a poor shepherd boy was standing in the road, begging to see him. The King commanded that the boy be brought before him, and Ios, trembling with joy, came to the side of the carriage and gazed long and steadfastly on the face he adored.

The King was amazed at this ardent look.

'Who are you?' he asked.

'Ios, the shepherd boy, my King.'

'What favour do you seek from me?' demanded the King.

Ios replied, 'O my King, all my life I have wished to see you. My greatest longing has been to look at your face, and now I have achieved my heart's desire. Happy and content, I can return to minding my sheep, forever blessed by having seen you!'

The King was greatly moved and looked long and earnestly at the boy before ordering the procession to continue.

Ios returned to his sheep and tended his flocks in perfect contentment and happiness, the memory of the King's face always fresh in his mind's eye.

The memory of his meeting with Ios stayed with the King too. He had never before seen such love and devotion. All those who surrounded him continually benefited from his favours and generosity but this shepherd boy had wanted and asked for nothing and was happy to live and die with just the memory of having seen his face.

We'll have more of this story tomorrow.

For Consultation

What do you think of this story? Can you compare this with any feelings you as a Bahá'í have?

DAY 6

A Prayer to Remember

Learn this portion of the prayer of 'Abdu'l-Bahá today:

> O Thou compassionate Lord! O Lord of Hosts! Praise be unto Thee that Thou hast preferred these young children over the full grown and the matured …

Activity

There is more to the story of Ios! Would you like to know it? Here it is …

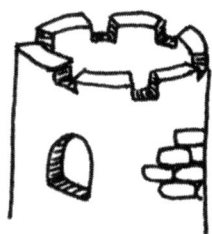

Ios and the King's Treasure

The memory of Ios haunted the King and his longing for the devoted shepherd grew so strong that at last he sent a messenger to summon the shepherd boy to the Royal Palace.

Unable to believe the good news, Ios came to the palace with eagerness and joy. Trembling with happiness he presented himself to the King.

The King was very pleased with Ios because Ios wanted nothing but to be near him. The King soon made him the guardian of his treasury, a position of great honour and responsibility.

But others who lived at the court of the King were jealous of the favour shown to Ios. They plotted together to try and find some fault with Ios so that they could destroy the King's trust in him. Day and night the courtiers kept watch on Ios and soon they found what they were seeking.

Each night, when everyone else was asleep, they would see Ios creep out of his room, stealthily wind his way through the corridors of the palace and climb the stairs to a small room at the top of one of the palace's many towers.

'Aha!' they whispered to themselves, 'he is robbing the King's treasure and storing it away secretly for himself.' And with glee, they hastened to take the news of their discovery to the King.

The King was angered and saddened at the news.

'I cannot believe this terrible thing you say of Ios,' he cried. 'Before I believe you I must see for myself if what you say is true.'

That night the King watched with the jealous courtiers. Sure enough, just as they had reported to him, Ios crept from his room and found his way to the small chamber in the tower. With sorrow the King followed and threw open the door of the little room with a mighty crash!

The room was completely bare and empty, except that on the wall hung the simple shepherd's coat which Ios had worn when he first met the King and the shepherd's crook he had used to tend his flock. Ios was sitting on the floor gazing at them.

'What is the meaning of this, Ios?' exclaimed the King, 'Why do you creep so quietly about my palace in the middle of the night, arousing my suspicions when I have raised you up and put my trust in you?'

'O my King,' replied Ios, 'when I first set my eyes on you I was a poor and ignorant shepherd boy. I have risen to this high position only through your bounty, favour and generosity. I wish never to forget what I was and from where I came so I may always remain humble and grateful to you. So, each night, I come here to think of what I was and what you, in your goodness and kindness, have made me.'

And the King marvelled at his fortune in having a servant as loyal and devoted as Ios.

Tomorrow we'll read more about Ios. By now you might like to draw a picture! How about drawing Ios when he meets the King? Would Ios be full of light? Would the King?

For Consultation

Why does the King appreciate Ios?

DAY 7

A Prayer to Remember

Learn more of the prayer today:

> O Thou compassionate Lord! O Lord of Hosts! Praise be unto Thee that Thou hast preferred these young children over the full grown and the matured, hast endowed them with Thy special bounty …

How is it coming along? Do you enjoy saying it? Never get overworked trying to learn it – enjoy what you can learn.

Activity

We will see today that Ios is sincerely devoted to his King. Here is another thought-provoking story.

Ios and the Melon

One day the King held a great feast and, as was the custom, invited many guests and plied them with all kinds of beautiful food and luscious fruit.

At last everything had gone except one specially ripe and

delicious-looking melon. Just then Ios, who had been away on important business for the King, returned.

Many of the guests started to murmur among themselves, 'You see, the King has been saving that delicious-looking melon and will give it to his favourite, Ios.'

Sure enough, the King, seating Ios by his side, ordered the melon to be cut in pieces and gave one to Ios, saying, 'You too, my faithful Ios, must share my feast. I have saved this melon just for you.'

Ios ate the slice of melon with obvious relish and the King gave him another and another, until, seeing the pleasure with which Ios ate, took the last piece himself, saying, 'I must taste for myself a little of this splendid fruit!'

However, no sooner had the King tasted the melon that he threw it down, exclaiming, 'This fruit is bitter as gall! How could you eat it, Ios? Did you not find it bitter to your taste?'

'Yes, indeed, O my King,' Ios replied, 'it was bitter and unpleasant. But as I have received from your hand so much that was sweet and pleasant, how could I refuse a little bitterness? Indeed, seeing that it was your hand that gave it to me, the melon's bitterness became sweetness itself in my mouth!'

For Consultation

I think Ios had a 'light' that was 'on' all the time. What do you think? How could he always be so content with the will of his King?

DAY 8

A Prayer to Remember

Memorize this portion of the prayer:

> O Thou compassionate Lord! O Lord of Hosts! Praise be unto Thee that Thou hast preferred these young children over the full grown and the matured, hast endowed them with Thy special bounty, hast guided them …

Activity

Please read more of Ios:

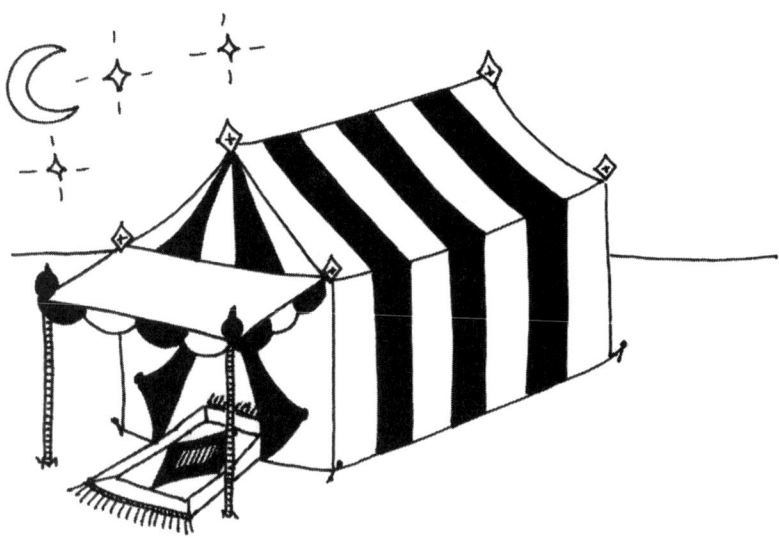

Ios and the Box of Jewels

Several years passed, and the King decided to go on a Royal Tour of his kingdom. Preparations started immediately and within a few days the magnificent procession was ready to leave. The ministers of the King's government, ambassadors and diplomats, courtiers and men of importance, soldiers and bandsmen, all splendid in their finery, set out to accompany the King. And, of course, the faithful Ios rode alongside his beloved master at the front of the throng.

Each evening the splendid party made camp and the wonderful imperial tent was erected for the King. This tent was the most beautiful and precious tent you have ever seen – woven from the finest silk, it was decorated with hundreds of jewels and precious stones, which so shone and sparkled in the lamp-light at night that the light of the moon and stars seemed to pale in comparison. Each night the King and his companions feasted and sang. Each morning, when the tent was struck, the jewels were collected and put in a box in the King's carriage.

Thus it was that the Royal Procession went on its way, the King looking contentedly at his peaceful and prosperous country, his followers happily riding and conversing during the day, and feasting and singing at night.

Then, one day, as the King and his retinue were making their way through some especially beautiful countryside, the King remembered that he had passed this way before. It had been on this very stretch of road, years ago, that he had first glanced upon the adoring face of his faithful Ios.

In gratitude for that meeting the King, seized of a sudden impulse, took the box of jewels and cast them on the road.

As the procession went on its way the King looked back to see all his followers, all except Ios, forgetful of their duty, scrambling on the ground in great confusion trying to gather up the precious stones.

'Look at Ios,' they muttered to each other, 'see how proud he is, he even despises the King's jewels and makes no effort to pick them up.'

'How is it Ios,' the King asked him, 'that you do not join the others to gather up my jewels? Are they not precious? Do you despise the very things that were mine?'

'O my King,' replied Ios, 'never in my life have I despised the least thing that is yours. But to be near you and gaze on your face has always been more than sufficient for me. Why should I leave your side to scramble for what you have thrown away?'

And the loyal and steadfast Ios rode on by the side of his grateful master, his gaze never for a moment leaving the face of his beloved King.

For Consultation

Here is a Hidden Word to consult on:

> O befriended Stranger! The candle of thine heart is lighted by the hand of My power, quench it not with the contrary winds of self and passion. The healer of all thine ills is remembrance of Me, forget it not. Make My love thy treasure and cherish it even as thy very sight and life.
>
> *Bahá'u'lláh*

Does Ios seem to serve his King in this way? Do we serve God in this way? Bahá'u'lláh asks us to serve like this.

DAY 9

A Prayer to Remember

Learn the prayer up to here by heart.

> O Thou compassionate Lord! O Lord of Hosts! Praise be unto Thee that Thou hast preferred these young children over the full grown and the matured, hast endowed them with Thy special bounty, hast guided them, hast bestowed upon them Thy Light and hast given them spirituality.

Activity

This is our last story of Ios. Enjoy!

The Passing of Ios

The thing that the King prized above all his other many splendid possessions throughout the length and breadth of his kingdom was the Royal Garden. This garden was vast and very beautiful with trees and flowers, still lakes, clear-flowing streams and fountains. Within the bounds of the garden every living creature was safe and protected, for it was forbidden for anyone to kill anything in the garden.

Now the King so loved and trusted Ios that he made him the guardian and custodian of this Garden of Life and Beauty, the highest honour the King could bestow. Ios guarded his trust faithfully.

The King's son was the only one throughout the realm whom the King loved more than Ios. The young prince was the apple of his father's eye and in his father's sight he could do no wrong.

Despite this, the prince was jealous of the trust and love that the King showed to Ios.

One day, as Ios was walking in the garden enjoying its beauty and ensuring that everything was as his royal master would wish, the young prince crept up stealthily behind Ios, and taking his bow, swiftly shot an arrow and as swiftly fled. The prince's arrow, true to his aim, struck down one of the royal swans. The blood flowed down the milky white breast into the clear water of the lake, and the swan swayed and drooped and died.

Ios stood horrified and grief-stricken, gazing first at the swan and then at the bow which had been thrown at his feet. As he stooped to pick up the bows one of the royal gardeners chanced by. Seeing Ios with the bow in his hand and the dead swan with its blood pinkly colouring the lake's pure water, he hastened straight away to tell the King what Ios had done.

The King summoned Ios to him.

'What have you done?' he demanded.

Ios bowed his head and remained silent.

'Speak!' the King commanded. 'Who killed the swan?'

But Ios, knowing the King's love for his son, would not answer.

Then, with a breaking heart, the King sternly exclaimed, 'Your silence condemns you. You have failed my trust. If you do not explain why you have done this terrible thing, I shall banish you forever from my presence.'

Silently, Ios lifted his eyes and took a long, last look at the face of his beloved King. Then he meekly bowed his head, went out from the presence of the King and went alone into exile.

Time passed and the prince's conscience gave him no rest. He saw how his father, the King, grieved for Ios, and he observed that his father's love for him was in no way increased with the departure of the former shepherd boy. Then the news reached him that Ios was dying of a broken heart in his lonely hut far away.

Full of remorse he went to the King and threw himself at his father's feet.

'Forgive me, father, for the wrong I have done you and Ios,' he cried. And he confessed all that he had done.

The King in great grief sprang to his feet and cried out, 'Take me at once to Ios!'

In all haste the King sped to the lonely, far away hut and found Ios dying. Rushing to him, the King clasped him in his arms while the tears flowed freely from the royal eyes.

'O Ios, my beloved servant and friend, you must not leave me: you are my most loved and trusted servant, you have sacrificed your happiness and life for the sake of me and my son!'

Ios, resting in the arms of his dearly-loved master and gazing once again on the face of the one he loved so much, exclaimed, 'O my King, my master! Never have I sought anything but your pleasure. Now, having gazed once more upon your noble face, I die happy and content in Paradise!' Saying which, he passed peacefully away.

For Consultation

Even in the most unhappy and unfair situation, the heart of Ios did not waver. To ensure what he thought was best for his King, he preferred his own unhappiness and went away. He gave his life to his beloved King: he lived for him and he died for him.

This story reminds me of the countless stories of Bahá'í martyrs – those Bahá'ís who gave up their lives in the service of the Faith of Bahá'u'lláh.

For an upcoming activity, please ask your teacher to select a story of one of the recent Bahá'í martyrs.

DAY 10

A Prayer to Remember

Try to memorize more of the prayer:

> O Thou compassionate Lord! O Lord of Hosts! Praise be unto Thee that Thou hast preferred these young children over the full grown and the matured, hast endowed them with Thy special bounty, hast guided them, hast bestowed upon them Thy Light and hast given them spirituality. Confirm us so that when we attain maturity …

Activity

One dictionary meaning of 'light' is 'a source of illumination, such as the sun or an electric lamp'.

Another definition is 'spiritual comprehension or awareness' and still another is 'to be born, come into existence'. Use your dictionary and together read through the many, many definitions of light.

For Consultation

Light is a very important word to us and has many meanings. We've talked about how light touches us inside – but what about outside? Does sunlight touch everyone on earth? Does one same sun touch everybody?

A Prayer to Remember

Today, read the whole prayer that you have been learning. Take the time to say it with a great deal of meaning and love.

Activity

Ask your teacher to read or tell you a story of a recent Bahá'í martyr. Stories of the Bahá'í martyrs teach us so much about love. But the martyrs also unfailingly shed light upon everyone who was involved with them. Many stories tell of gaolers, neighbours, officials or workmates who were very moved by the Bahá'í who was to give his life. Even in this way, divine light was shed and although people suffered, others became aware and learned about the Cause of God.

DAY 12

A Prayer to Remember

Memorize this portion of the prayer:

> O Thou compassionate Lord! O Lord of Hosts! Praise be unto Thee that Thou hast preferred these young children over the full grown and the matured, hast endowed them with Thy special bounty, hast guided them, hast bestowed upon them Thy Light and hast given them spirituality. Confirm us so that when we attain maturity we may be enabled to serve Thy kingdom …

Activity

Light a candle under the supervision of your teacher — or an adult, if your teacher is very young! Watch the flame of the candle. Sit peacefully and relax. Don't pay attention to anything else around you — just watch the flame. When you feel you have had enough, blow out the candle.

For Consultation

Talk about your activity. As the flame burns, what happens to the candle? When you blow it out, where does it go?

DAY 13

A Prayer to Remember

Memorize the prayer up to here:

> O Thou compassionate Lord! O Lord of Hosts! Praise be unto Thee that Thou hast preferred these young children over the full grown and the matured, hast endowed them with Thy special bounty, hast guided them, hast bestowed upon them Thy Light and hast given them spirituality. Confirm us so that when we attain maturity we may be enabled to serve Thy kingdom, may train the souls, may become ignited candles …

Activity

Have you ever seen a picture of the sun shining on the different religions in the world? Try to draw one yourself.

For Consultation

How can people see 'light'? Do they need religion? Can religions be all that different if they come from one God?

DAY 14

A Prayer to Remember

If you can learn this portion of the prayer, you will know nearly all of it.

> O Thou compassionate Lord! O Lord of Hosts! Praise be unto Thee that Thou hast preferred these young children over the full grown and the matured, hast endowed them with Thy special bounty, hast guided them, hast bestowed upon them Thy Light and hast given them spirituality. Confirm us so that when we attain maturity we

may be enabled to serve Thy kingdom, may train the souls, may become ignited candles and may shine like unto stars.

Activity
Bahá'u'lláh was born in the province of Núr (Light). Draw a picture of what that place might look like. Note: Out of respect for a Manifestation of God, we don't draw Bahá'u'lláh.

For Consultation
What would it be like to live in a place that was light all the time?

A Prayer to Remember
Can you say the prayer you have been learning by covering the words. Perhaps you still need to take a peek?

Activity
Go through your personal Bahá'í library and find some 'light' reading for tonight.

For Consultation
Why do people usually sleep in the dark at nighttime?

A Prayer to Remember
Read the whole prayer you have been learning. Do you ever practise it before you go to sleep?

Activity

Prepare a menu that you can serve your parents for tomorrow night's dinner. Keep it simple: consult with your teacher.

For Consultation

What will you need from the market?

A Prayer to Remember

Can you say the prayer by covering the words? Perhaps you needed fewer peeks today?

Activity

Prepare dinner (with help where needed). At dinner, as you serve, remember the feeling of Ios for his King. Can you serve your family with that special devotion?

A Prayer to Remember

Say the prayer you have been learning. Did you need to peek at all today?

Activity

Record 'minutes' of your dinner. Was it a success?

For Consultation

Ask your teacher to discuss this activity during report time at Feast. After all, this is quite an accomplishment!

DAY 19

A Prayer to Remember

How well did you learn 'Abdu'l-Bahá s beautiful prayer this month? Say the whole prayer by heart.

Tomorrow is the Feast of Mercy! You have done very well during the month of Light.

Activity for the Teacher

Please make a lovely award for your student and perhaps list the accomplishments of this child in Núr.

For Consultation

What will you want to accomplish in Raḥmat (Mercy)?

6

Month of Raḥmat (Mercy)

A Prayer

This month we will read and share different verses from prayers rather than memorize one prayer.

> Grant me then Thy sufficing help so as to make me independent of all things, O Thou Who art unsurpassed in Thy mercy!
>
> *The Báb*

Activity

Write a short story about a time when you feel someone (perhaps mum or dad or a teacher or friend) showed you 'mercy'.

For Consultation

Discuss the possibilities of what would happen if God were not merciful to us?

DAY 2

A Prayer

Grant me then Thy sufficing help so as to make me independent of all things, O Thou Who art unsurpassed in Thy mercy!

The Báb

Activity

Perform a skit! Be a merciful parent who has found his child doing something that he feels is wrong. Could your teacher be the child in the skit?

For Consultation

Take a minute to comment on the feelings expressed by the parent and the child. Was the situation resolved? How did it feel to be 'merciful'?

DAY 3

A Reading

Grant me then Thy sufficing help so as to make me independent of all things, O Thou Who art unsurpassed in Thy mercy!

The Báb

Activity

Paint a picture of your idea of 'mercy'.

For Consultation

If God never showed 'mercy' and only showed 'justice', what would happen?

DAY 4

A Reading

The eye of the mercy of Him Who is the Desire of the worlds is turned towards all men.

Bahá'u'lláh

Activity

Write a list of all the things about you that you would love God to know.

For Consultation

How does God know things about us?

DAY 5

A Reading

The eye of the mercy of Him Who is the Desire of the worlds is turned towards all men.

Bahá'u'lláh

Activity

Today write a list of a few things that perhaps you wish God could help you change about yourself.

For Consultation

How do your two lists from yesterday and today compare? Do they give you a clear idea of the direction you can take to make yourself happier with yourself? Will others be happier with you too?

A Reading

The eye of the mercy of Him Who is the Desire of the worlds is turned towards all men.

Bahá'u'lláh

Activity

Ask your parents or teacher to tell you things they find very positive … good … wonderful about you. Make one 'resolution' that you can work on this month in order to test yourself. (For instance, I won't bite my nails, hit my sister, eat huge bites of food …)

DAY 7

A Prayer

Thy mercy to me is my healing and my succour in both this world and the world to come.

Bahá'u'lláh

Activity

What does 'mercy' mean? Look it up in the dictionary.

Because you just did so much work to look up 'mercy' in the dictionary and you learned about it, I am going to show 'mercy' to you and let you go play now!

(If you would rather learn more, then have a consultation on a subject of your choice today!)

DAY 8

A Prayer

Thy mercy to me is my healing and my succour in both this world and the world to come.

Bahá'u'lláh

Activity

Do you have your play dough ready? If so, build all the little animals you would take care of if you were a merciful shepherd.

For Consultation

Remember the stories of Ios? Would Ios have been a merciful shepherd?

DAY 9

A Reading

Thy mercy to me is my healing and my succour in both this world and the world to come.

Bahá'u'lláh

Activity

When you take a walk, do you squash ants or other 'bugs' on the footpath? Do you try to avoid them and let them live? Take a walk and see.

For Consultation

What happened on your walk? Did 'bugs' get automatically squashed or did you make a choice? Did you try very hard not to walk on any? Why? Does everything you do have a reason?

DAY 10

A Prayer

O God! Thou art more friend to me than I am to myself. I dedicate myself to Thee, O Lord.

'Abdu'l-Bahá

Activity

Today tie a little string around your finger. When someone asks, 'Why do you have that string on your finger?' you can say, 'Because it reminds me to be friendly to everyone!' Make a special effort.

For Consultation

Being happy all the time is a good thing. Why is that?

A Prayer

Read this prayer again with a great deal of feeling.

> O God! Thou art more friend to me than I am to myself. I dedicate myself to Thee, O Lord.
>
> *'Abdu'l-Bahá*

Activity

The Feast of Kalimát (Words) is coming next. Would you and your teacher like to think of something really friendly to do for your friends at the Feast? Don't tell me what it is now … surprise me! I can't wait!

For Consultation

Have a talk about the string you wore yesterday. Did anyone ask you what it was? What did you say and what did it remind you to do? Did it work?

DAY 12

A Prayer

O God! Thou art more friend to me than I am to myself. I dedicate myself to Thee, O Lord.

'Abdu'l-Bahá

Activity

What are your five favourite things about being a Bahá'í? Do you feel very lucky?

For Consultation

Discuss the fact that Bahá'u'lláh came from God to teach us about unity. Do you need to be friendly with people before you can be united with them?

DAY 13

A Prayer

O my Lord! O my Lord!
   I am a child of tender years. Nourish me from the breast of Thy mercy, train me in the bosom of Thy love …

'Abdu'l-Bahá

Activity

Write another letter today to your pen pal and tell him or her all your news.

For Consultation

What do you think will happen before we have world unity? How will people need to change? Have any of the changes you have tried to make in yourself worked?

A Prayer

O my Lord! O my Lord!
  I am a child of tender years. Nourish me from the breast of Thy mercy, train me in the bosom of Thy love …

'Abdu'l-Bahá

Activity

If you have building blocks or anything like them, try to build a nine-pointed star. This is sometimes used as a symbol of the Bahá'í Faith. Experiment and make some pretty shapes.

For Consultation

Did you know that Bahá'í Houses of Worship have nine sides? Do you know why?

DAY 15

A Prayer

O my Lord! O my Lord!

I am a child of tender years. Nourish me from the breast of Thy mercy, train me in the bosom of Thy love …

'Abdu'l-Bahá

Activity

Can you draw a picture of your idea for a Bahá'í House of Worship?

For Consultation

What do you like about the Temple you have drawn? Where do you imagine it is located?

DAY 16

A Prayer

O my God! O my God! Verily, I invoke Thee and supplicate before Thy threshold asking Thee that all Thy mercies may descend upon these souls.

'Abdu'l-Bahá

Activity

Find some old magazines or newspapers and cut out pictures of things you like in the world. You'll have to look carefully!

For Consultation

What are the most important things you are looking for? Are lots of people in the pictures?

DAY 17

A Prayer

O my God! O my God! Verily, I invoke Thee and supplicate before Thy threshold asking Thee that all Thy mercies may descend upon these souls.

'Abdu'l-Bahá

Activity

Continue looking for pictures. Find a big poster board or some construction paper.

For Consultation

Talk with your teacher about which picture you like the very most and why. You will see why tomorrow.

DAY 18

A Prayer

O my God! O my God! Verily, I invoke Thee and supplicate before Thy threshold asking Thee that all Thy mercies may descend upon these souls.

'Abdu'l-Bahá

Activity

Gather all the cut-outs and the poster board. Now with a dab of glue you can make an important poster to keep or give. Your favourite picture could go in the middle and coming out from this could be pictures placed in the design of the nine-pointed star. Decorate the star with all the pictures and then draw in a pretty colour around the outside so that the star shape is easy to see. Would you like to show this to your friends?

DAY 19

A Prayer

O my God! O my God! Verily, I invoke Thee and supplicate before Thy threshold asking Thee that all Thy mercies may descend upon these souls.

'Abdu'l-Bahá

Activity

You have learned a lot about mercy now. You have also learned about unity! Here is a little story about unity.

Long ago there lived a wise old man who owned a large farm and had many sons. It was his greatest wish that before he died they would work successfully and happily together to make the farm prosperous and flourishing, but alas, they were always fighting and arguing amongst themselves. Because of this the once beautiful fields and vineyards were badly neglected and indeed nothing seemed to turn out right, simply because they just could not work together in unity. One day in despair their father sent for them and told them each to bring a single stick. When they arrived he took the sticks and had them bound together into a bundle. Giving the bundle to his sons, he asked each in turn to attempt to break it in two. They all struggled but none was strong enough to perform the feat. Then the old man had the bundle untied and gave a single stick to each of his sons and asked them to try again. This time the sticks broke easily. The sons wondered greatly at the meaning of this test until their father explained to them that if they were united they would be like the bundle of sticks: strong and able to withstand great pressures, especially from their enemies. If they continued to be divided like the single sticks, then they would just as easily break and fail.

For Consultation

Is unity important? Have a lovely Nineteen Day Feast!

7
Month of Kalimát (Words)

DAY 1

A Prayer to Remember

Bless Thou, O Lord my God, Him Whom Thou hast set over Thy most excellent Titles, and through Whom Thou hast divided between the godly and the wicked, and graciously aid us to do what Thou lovest and desirest. Bless Thou, moreover, O my God, them Who are Thy Words and Thy Letters, and them who have set their faces towards Thee and turned unto Thy face, and hearkened to Thy Call.

Bahá'u'lláh

Activity

This is a long and beautiful prayer. Try to read it every day this month. You will become more familiar with it every time you read it. It will mean more to you every time if you concentrate on the message.

For Consultation
For a short period of time (say half an hour) do not say a word. Find alternative methods of communication.

During that period did you laugh with other people, did you get frustrated? Did you use sign language? What do you think of this experience?

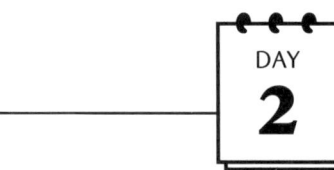

A Prayer to Remember
Say the prayer you said yesterday.

Activity
Start a list of what you consider to be the most basic words we use.

For Consultation
Why does God send His word through a Prophet?

A Prayer to Remember
Learn this portion of the prayer:

> Bless Thou, O Lord my God, Him Whom Thou hast set over Thy most excellent Titles …

Activity
Continue your list of words. Now include those you consider necessary to express yourself better.

For Consultation

The dictionary says a word can be 'a command or direction; an order'. Discuss this. Has your opinion of why God sends His word through a Prophet, as you discussed yesterday, changed? (How could we understand the message without it being given to us in words?)

A Prayer to Remember

Bless Thou, O Lord my God, Him Whom Thou hast set over Thy most excellent Titles …

Activity

Try this little exercise. When your teacher reads a word out loud, you say what comes to your mind.

Car	Work	Picnic
Tomato	Evening	Ball
Kitchen	Knit	Mind
Finish	TV	

For Consultation

What do words make you do automatically? Do they cause you to think? Do you think along with the person who is talking?

DAY 5

A Prayer to Remember

Memorize this portion of the prayer:

> Bless Thou, O Lord my God, Him Whom Thou hast set over Thy most excellent Titles, and through Whom Thou hast divided between the godly and the wicked …

Activity

The story of the tower of Babel can be found in the Bible (Genesis:11:1–9). Descendants of Noah built a tower in ancient Babylonia which they intended to reach up to heaven. The story goes that this angered God. He caused a mass confusion amongst the builders by changing their language into many different languages and then scattered the people all over the earth. The English word 'babble' comes from this story. What would a tower going up to heaven look like?

For Consultation

Do you have a friend who speaks a different language from you? How do you manage to communicate?

A Prayer to Remember

Bless Thou, O Lord my God, Him Whom Thou hast set over Thy most excellent Titles, and through Whom Thou hast divided between the godly and the wicked …

Activity

Play-act with your teacher using make-believe languages. Pretend you need to find a friend who lives at 44 Pine Street and you don't know how to get there. Have fun!

For Consultation

Were you babbling when you spoke your make-believe language? Did it sound funny and make you laugh?

A Prayer to Remember

Memorize the prayer up to here:

Bless Thou, O Lord my God, Him Whom Thou hast set over

Thy most excellent Titles, and through Whom Thou hast divided between the godly and the wicked, and graciously aid us to do what Thou lovest and desirest.

Activity

Listen to some Bahá'í music and dance or move to it.

For Consultation

Do we all understand music even if the words sound funny?

A Prayer to Remember

Bless Thou, O Lord my God, Him Whom Thou hast set over Thy most excellent Titles, and through Whom Thou hast divided between the godly and the wicked, and graciously aid us to do what Thou lovest and desirest.

A Reading

The essence of faith is fewness of words and abundance of deeds; he whose words exceed his deeds, know verily his death is better than his life.

Bahá'u'lláh

For Consultation

Talk about a good deed you have performed. When we grow close to God, we want everything we do to be acceptable and a 'good deed'!

DAY 9

A Prayer to Remember

Bless Thou, O Lord my God, Him Whom Thou hast set over Thy most excellent Titles, and through Whom Thou hast divided between the godly and the wicked, and graciously aid us to do what Thou lovest and desirest.

Activity

When Bahá'u'lláh uses words from God, they become commands to us, His followers, to obey. Some words are laws, which we must follow exactly. Other words give us direction and purpose and unity but give us lots of choices. It is important to learn from these words.

For Consultation

Discuss the tools we have for learning from Bahá'u'lláh (i.e. heart, love, feelings, example, etc.)

DAY 10

A Prayer to Remember

Bless Thou, O Lord my God, Him Whom Thou hast set over Thy most excellent Titles, and through Whom Thou hast divided between the godly and the wicked, and graciously aid us to do what Thou lovest and desirest. Bless Thou, moreover, O my God …

Activity

The quotation we read on Day 8 says that our deeds are worth more than many words which talk about our faith. Write a list of things you could do as a Bahá'í to make your life special and helpful to others.

For Consultation
Do words mean different things to different people?

DAY 11

A Prayer to Remember
> Bless Thou, O Lord my God, Him Whom Thou hast set over Thy most excellent Titles, and through Whom Thou hast divided between the godly and the wicked, and graciously aid us to do what Thou lovest and desirest. Bless Thou, moreover, O my God …

Activity
There are so many things to learn about Bahá'u'lláh and His life. Listen to this:

> From Adrianople, and later from 'Akká, Bahá'u'lláh addressed the rulers of the world in a series of Letters. To them He declared His Divine Mission, and called them to serve peace, justice and righteousness. The majestic sweep of His counsel and admonition revealed in these letters, arrests the deepest attention of every earnest student of the Bahá'í Faith.
>
> H.M. Balyuzi

For Consultation
We see that Bahá'u'lláh wrote to the leaders of the world to tell them of God's message. Did they listen? What did Bahá'u'lláh tell them? (Read it above.)

A Prayer to Remember

Bless Thou, O Lord my God, Him Whom Thou hast set over Thy most excellent Titles, and through Whom Thou hast divided between the godly and the wicked, and graciously aid us to do what Thou lovest and desirest. Bless Thou, moreover, O my God, them Who are Thy Words and Thy Letters …

Activity

Write a letter which you would send to the rulers of your country to tell them about Bahá'u'lláh. How would you explain the Bahá'í Faith?

For Consultation

There are Bahá'ís in every country who have the responsibility of presenting or proclaiming the Bahá'í Faith to that country's leaders and dignitaries. Even in our own towns we proclaim the Faith to the leaders of the town. Perhaps your Assembly or parents or friends have done this where you live. Have they? Is there anything you can do to help?

DAY 13

A Prayer to Remember

Bless Thou, O Lord my God, Him Whom Thou hast set over Thy most excellent Titles, and through Whom Thou hast divided between the godly and the wicked, and graciously aid us to do what Thou lovest and desirest. Bless Thou, moreover, O my God, them Who are Thy Words and Thy Letters …

Activity

Read this prayer and look up the words you don't know in the dictionary.

All-praise be to the one true God – exalted be His glory – inasmuch as He hath, through the Pen of the Most High, unlocked the doors of men's hearts. Every verse which this Pen hath revealed is a bright and shining portal that discloseth the glories of a saintly and pious life, of pure and stainless deeds. The summons and the message which We gave were never intended to reach or to benefit one land or one people only. Mankind in its entirety must firmly adhere to whatsoever hath been revealed and vouchsafed unto it. Then and only then will it attain unto true liberty. The whole earth is illuminated with the resplendent glory of God's Revelation.

Bahá'u'lláh

For Consultation

Does humanity need to know what Bahá'u'lláh has said?

A Prayer to Remember

Bless Thou, O Lord my God, Him Whom Thou hast set over Thy most excellent Titles, and through Whom Thou hast divided between the godly and the wicked, and graciously aid us to do what Thou lovest and desirest. Bless Thou, moreover, O my God, them Who are Thy Words and Thy Letters, and them who have set their faces towards Thee …

Activity

The tongue I have designed for the mention of Me …

Bahá'u'lláh

Tie a string around your finger. If people ask you why you are wearing it, tell them that you have promised yourself not to say one single word about anybody that wasn't good. Wear the string for a whole day.

For Consultation

Discuss today's reading and find it in *The Hidden Words*. Maybe you have the time to read from this book.

A Prayer to Remember

Learn the prayer up to here – you are nearly at the end!

Bless Thou, O Lord my God, Him Whom Thou hast set over Thy most excellent Titles, and through Whom Thou hast divided between the godly and the wicked, and graciously aid us to do what Thou lovest and desirest. Bless Thou, moreover, O my God, them

Who are Thy Words and Thy Letters, and them who have set their faces towards Thee and turned unto Thy face …

Activity

Hearken to the delightsome words of My honeyed tongue, and quaff the stream of mystic holiness from My sugar-shedding lips.

Bahá'u'lláh

The above reading is an example of the beauty created by the words of Bahá'u'lláh. You may not understand exactly what is being said, but do you feel the beauty and love? With some paints, use your brush and colour to express the feeling of this reading. If it turns out to be a nice piece of work, you could write the words on it and have a treasure to keep.

For Consultation

Ask your teacher or parents if they treasure the words of Bahá'u'lláh. Ask them why.

DAY 16

A Prayer to Remember

Repeat the whole prayer:

Bless Thou, O Lord my God, Him Whom Thou hast set over Thy most excellent Titles, and through Whom Thou hast divided between the godly and the wicked, and graciously aid us to do what Thou lovest and desirest. Bless Thou, moreover, O my God, them Who are Thy Words and Thy Letters, and them who have set their faces towards Thee and turned unto Thy face, and hearkened to Thy Call.

Bahá'u'lláh

Activity

Find a Hidden Word you would like to read today and read it to your teacher. The dictionary says a word is a 'command or direction: an order'. Pretend you are driving a car and reading the road signs. Maybe your teacher can call out some directions, too, to make your drive really exciting.

For Consultation

How would people drive with no road signs, no direction signs and no understanding of how to work a car? Can you compare that situation to living without the word of God?

DAY 17

A Prayer to Remember

Say the whole prayer you have learned.

Activity

When you recite a prayer with love bursting in your heart and your face turned to God, you have made yourself a happier person and also reached out to the souls of other people. It is one way to help make the whole world a happier place, isn't it?

Read this passage:

> Whoso reciteth, in the privacy of his chamber, the verses revealed by God, the scattering angels of the Almighty shall scatter abroad the fragrance of the words uttered by his mouth, and shall cause the heart of every righteous man to throb.
>
> *Bahá'u'lláh*

For Consultation

Do you realize that you have just done a great deed for humankind? Talk about it.

DAY 18

A Prayer to Remember
Please say the prayer again and remember God every second.

Activity
Sing a Bahá'í song that you know. You might even want to sing a few of them.

For Consultation
Do you feel happy? I hope so!

DAY 19

A Prayer to Remember
This is the last day of Kalimát (Words) for this year. Please say the prayer you have memorized one more time.

Activity
Write a short talk to give to your family tonight. Tell them about words and the word of God. Tell them how important it is to remember the word of God and what it does for everyone.

For Consultation
Give your teacher a comforting hug! Decide together whether or not you have learned a lot this month.

8

Month of Kamál
(Perfection)

A Reading to Remember

Love the creatures for the sake of God and not for themselves. You will never become angry or impatient if you love them for the sake of God. Humanity is not perfect. There are imperfections in every human being, and you will always become unhappy if you look toward the people themselves. But if you look toward God, you will love them and be kind to them, for the world of God is the world of perfection and complete mercy. Therefore, do not look at the shortcomings of anybody; see with the sight of forgiveness.

'Abdu'l-Bahá

Activity

Welcome to the 19 days of Kamál! It is a perfect month; well, it is the month of 'perfection'. Just for starters, you'll need a little mirror. Or go to a mirror for a few moments. Have a look at yourself. What do you see? Do you like your face? Can you see any of your character? Do you look happy, shy, comical or just wonderfully gorgeous?

For Consultation

Do you think you are what you appear to be? Is your face a reflection of you?

A Reading to Remember

Learn these words of 'Abdu'l-Bahá by heart:

> Love the creatures for the sake of God and not for themselves.

Activity

Write down the names of everybody in your family and also people you know well. Next to each name write the thing you like best about that person.

For Consultation

Discuss what characteristics you like the best in people.

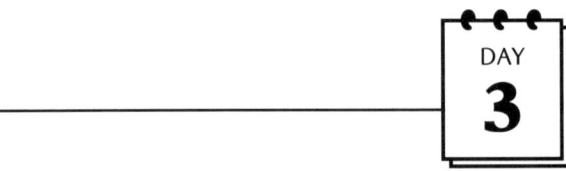

A Reading to Remember

> Love the creatures for the sake of God and not for themselves.

Activity

Draw a picture of how you look when you are angry. Draw other people looking angry. Is it nice?

For Consultation

Do you think people change their feelings a lot? Is it easy to know how other people are feeling all the time?

A Reading to Remember

Learn this portion of the reading by heart:

> Love the creatures for the sake of God and not for themselves. You will never become angry or impatient if you love them for the sake of God.

Activity

Try this skit: You be an angry old man. Your teacher can be a happy old man. Sit down on a park bench together and talk. Try to make both men happy.

For Consultation

Discuss the way you had to try to talk to make the men happy. Were you successful? What did you learn?

DAY 5

A Reading to Remember

Love the creatures for the sake of God and not for themselves. You will never become angry or impatient if you love them for the sake of God.

Activity

Ask your parents tonight if there is a special way parents love their children that enables parents to love their children all the time. Parents don't only love their children when they are pleasant; they also love them at those times when they are very difficult to get along with. Ask your parents how this can be. Let them tell you how they felt when you were a baby and what they think of you now.

For Consultation

Your consultation is: Do you love your parents all the time?

DAY 6

A Reading to Remember

Learn more of the passage from 'Abdu'l-Bahá:

Love the creatures for the sake of God and not for themselves. You will never become angry or impatient if you love them for the sake of God. Humanity is not perfect.

Activity

According to Bahá'u'lláh, God created us because He loved us and has created us all the same way. Tie a string on your finger today. When anyone asks you what it's for you can say you want to be friends with everyone and to see the best in everyone.

For Consultation

When people think we are capable of great things, it gives us the support we need to be able to do them. If we see things only in very limited ways, that is usually as far as we try; that is, we don't really try at all. This happens in many different ways. Can you talk about this and come to a conclusion?

DAY 7

A Reading to Remember

Learn the passage up to here:

> Love the creatures for the sake of God and not for themselves. You will never become angry or impatient if you love them for the sake of God. Humanity is not perfect. There are imperfections in every human being …

Activity

Write down in your diary (I hope you're still working on it) what happened when you wore the string yesterday. Did people notice your effort? Was it sincere? Can you get along with people when you try?

For Consultation

Do people sometimes expect too much of you? Consult on ways to work this out.

DAY 8

A Reading to Remember
More of the passage to learn.

> Love the creatures for the sake of God and not for themselves. You will never become angry or impatient if you love them for the sake of God. Humanity is not perfect. There are imperfections in every human being, and you will always become unhappy if you look toward the people themselves.

Activity

'Abdu'l-Bahá saw everyone in a positive light. He said, 'O ye friends! Fellowship, fellowship! Love, love! Unity, unity! – So that the power of the Bahá'í Cause may appear and become manifest in the world of existence.' He went on to say that if we understood how powerful is the love between us, we would all be in love with each other!

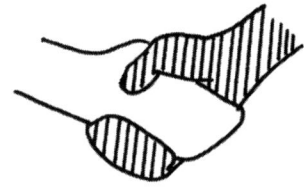

Think about the above statement.

For Consultation
What happens when we don't care much for each other?

DAY 9

A Reading to Remember
Try to memorize these words:

> Love the creatures for the sake of God and not for themselves. You will never become angry or impatient if you love them for the

sake of God. Humanity is not perfect. There are imperfections in every human being, and you will always become unhappy if you look toward the people themselves. But if you look toward God, you will love them and be kind to them …

Activity

Draw a picture entitled 'Fellowship, Love, Unity!' Take it to Feast, where you can present it with love.

For Consultation

What does 'Fellowship, Love, Unity' mean to you?

DAY 10

A Reading to Remember

When you learn these words, you will have memorized nearly the whole passage:

> Love the creatures for the sake of God and not for themselves. You will never become angry or impatient if you love them for the sake of God. Humanity is not perfect. There are imperfections in every human being, and you will always become unhappy if you look toward the people themselves. But if you look toward God, you will love them and be kind to them, for the world of God is the world of perfection and complete mercy.

Activity

Stand up and jump for a few minutes. Loosen up your body and shake yourself. If you feel like laughing, that's terrific! Give your head a nice massage, rub all your fingers and toes and bend backward as far as you can safely! Jump like a little kangaroo, run like a pig, beg like a dog and meow happily like a kitten.

For Consultation

If we make a mistake and everything goes wrong, what can we do? (Pray and change our actions.)

A Reading to Remember

Love the creatures for the sake of God and not for themselves. You will never become angry or impatient if you love them for the sake of God. Humanity is not perfect. There are imperfections in every human being, and you will always become unhappy if you look toward the people themselves. But if you look toward God, you will love them and be kind to them, for the world of God is the world of perfection and complete mercy.

Activity

Write a short poem about how mistakes happen. Write another poem about being friends with everyone. Read the poems to your teacher and make any changes.

A Reading to Remember

Love the creatures for the sake of God and not for themselves. You will never become angry or impatient if you love them for the sake of God. Humanity is not perfect. There are imperfections in every human being, and you will always become unhappy if you look toward the people themselves. But if you look toward God, you will love them and be kind to them, for the world of God is the world of perfection and complete mercy.

Activity

Cut out your poems and stick them in your diary.

For Consultation

Consult on how everyone in the world really needs the same things.

DAY 13

A Reading to Remember

Say the whole reading.

> Love the creatures for the sake of God and not for themselves. You will never become angry or impatient if you love them for the sake of God. Humanity is not perfect. There are imperfections in every human being, and you will always become unhappy if you look toward the people themselves. But if you look toward God, you will love them and be kind to them, for the world of God is the world of perfection and complete mercy. Therefore, do not look at the shortcomings of anybody; see with the sight of forgiveness.
>
> — 'Abdu'l-Bahá

Activity

Go outside and look at the beautiful nature that surrounds you. Do you see the beauty? It is much better than seeing something that doesn't look so nice. This is like the world of God – a beautiful garden where you are happy and feel perfect. Can you draw that?

For Consultation

In the world of humanity we have to expect mistakes. It is better to forgive our mistakes than to be continually unhappy because of them. Discuss this.

A Reading to Remember

Now you have learned the whole passage. Recite it without peeking, if you can.

Activity

Seek permission to plant a tree. Because you have just learned a wonderful lesson of life, plant a tree to remember it always. It will also bring more life to the world! If you can't plant it now, try to get one and look after it until it can be planted.

For Consultation

Did Bahá'u'lláh forgive the world for all the hardship of His life? Is that a perfect lesson for us?

A Reading

By the righteousness of the one true God! If one speck of a jewel be lost and buried beneath a mountain of stones, and lie hidden beyond the seven seas, the Hand of Omnipotence would assuredly reveal it in this Day, pure and cleansed from dross.

Bahá'u'lláh

Activity

Get out your play dough and make some jewels. Think about hiding the jewels in the lounge and tonight you can ask the family to join in a search to find them! You can also make some paper rings or whatever you think would look pretty.

For Consultation

Every time a jewel is found we get a special feeling. When we love each other it is like having lots of jewels. Do you agree with that?

A Reading

Ye are the fruits of one tree, and the leaves of one branch.

Bahá'u'lláh

Activity

Find a special little box that you can use as a treasure chest. In it you could keep the things (like a few of the jewels) that will always remind you of each unique jewel of humankind.

For Consultation

In what ways are we all fruits of one tree or leaves of one branch?

DAY 17

A Prayer

O Thou forgiving Lord! Thou art the shelter of all these Thy servants. Thou knowest the secrets and art aware of all things.
'Abdu'l-Bahá

Activity

Spend a few moments by yourself telling God all your secrets. Then sit quietly and think happy thoughts.

For Consultation

When you obey your parents are you obeying God? Is God like a parent to everybody?

DAY 18

A Prayer

O God! Refresh and gladden my spirit. Purify my heart. Illumine my powers. I lay all my affairs in Thy hand. Thou art my Guide and my Refuge. I will no longer be sorrowful and grieved; I will be a happy and joyful being.

'Abdu'l-Bahá

Activity

Spend a few moments by yourself again. You are a child of God. Is that exciting? Everyone is! You are going to have a wonderful lifetime to learn about pleasing God. Is that special? Do you want to feel that happy about everyone else too? Sure you do! So sit and reflect on the purpose of your life.

For Consultation

In school we find a lot of our hidden talents. You might be great at maths or reading. Talk about your talents and ask your teacher to help you think what you can do with them.

DAY 19

A Reading

For the last day of Kamál (Perfection) read from *The Hidden Words*:

> O Son of Man! I loved thy creation, hence I created thee. Wherefore, do thou love Me, that I may name thy name and fill thy soul with the spirit of life.

Bahá'u'lláh

Activity

Make a list of all the people you will remember when you say your daily prayers. If you want to add a name or two occasionally, that's great!

For Consultation

Have a cool drink and chat with your teacher. What a perfect team!

9

Month of Asmá' (Names)

DAY 1

A Prayer to Remember

During the month of Names learn this prayer of the Báb by heart. Recite it each day.

> Magnified be Thy Name, O God, Thou art the King, the Eternal Truth; Thou knowest what is in the heavens and on the earth, and unto Thee must all return.
>
> *The Báb*

Activity

Do you have a magnifying glass? Find it and try it out on various items. Find shiny things, living things, wooden things, metal things, paper, words, food, etc.

For Consultation

When you magnify an object what happens to your view of it? Why in your opinion does the Báb pray that the name of God be magnified?

DAY 2

A Prayer to Remember

Magnified be Thy Name, O God, Thou art the King, the Eternal Truth; Thou knowest what is in the heavens and on the earth, and unto Thee must all return.

The Báb

How much have you learned by heart?

Activity

The dictionary defines a name or names as 'a word by which a person, place or thing is known or called'. A name can also be a title. Bahá'u'lláh is 'the Glory of God'. What other names can you think of who were Prophets of God?

For Consultation

What does a name mean to you? Are people different because of their names?

A Prayer to Remember

Read carefully the words of the prayer you are learning.

Activity

Names are sometimes used to label a characteristic of a person, place or thing. In some countries people are named for one of their characteristics such as 'Rose', 'Happy Hunter', 'Tiny Sparrow' or 'Red'. Draw some people and give them names.

For Consultation

Do you like your name? Why or why not?

A Prayer to Remember

Magnified be Thy Name, O God, Thou art the King, the Eternal Truth …

Have you remembered the first line yet?

Activity

Towns and cities have names. Think of 'Spring Brook'; does it sound pretty?

How about 'Alice Springs'? Some places are named for people or are given the same name as a much-loved home far away, for example Washington DC or Newcastle. Of course, the list is endless. Have a look at the names of towns in your area on a map.

For Consultation
Talk about names for towns that you would like to see.

DAY 5

A Prayer to Remember
> Magnified be Thy Name, O God, Thou art the King, the Eternal Truth …

Activity
Make a map of a make-believe place using the names you thought of yesterday.

For Consultation
What are names for? Do names help keep directions clear and help our understanding of who is who and where is where? Without names, I think we would be using incomplete signals.

A Prayer to Remember

Magnified be Thy Name, O God, Thou art the King, the Eternal Truth …

Activity

Things have names. If I wanted your ball I would say, 'I want your ball please.' If there was no name for 'ball', I would not be able to communicate unless I grabbed the round bouncing globe you were holding. What a mess! To demonstrate, act these out:

> Pass me the salt please.
> Where is your car?
> The dog wants in.
> Can you play the violin?

For Consultation

Is language important? Would it be wonderful to have a language the whole population could share?

A Prayer to Remember

Can you remember the prayer up to here?

> Magnified be Thy Name, O God, Thou art the King, the Eternal Truth; Thou knowest what is in the heavens and on the earth …

Activity

Let's play that game we played yesterday again. Act out:

Show me your smile.
Where is your heart?
I can dance.
I love you.
You are an angel!

For Consultation

Where does the understanding of a name come from? Some names make you feel happy, some sad, some thoughtful; some sound powerful and on and on. Why do we get so many feelings from names?

DAY 8

A Prayer to Remember

Magnified be Thy Name, O God, Thou art the King, the Eternal Truth; Thou knowest what is in the heavens and on the earth …

Activity

See if you can find any books by Bahá'u'lláh on your bookshelf. Bahá'u'lláh wrote many books (over a hundred) and many of them are in different styles. You have read from *The Hidden Words* which has short passages of encouragement to help us with our behaviour. *The Seven Valleys* and *The Four Valleys* are mystical essays and are best understood by our hearts. The Kitáb-i-Aqdas is the Book of Laws and is Bahá'u'lláh's Most Holy Book. These are all different and I hope you will read them.

For Consultation

If someone asked you what was the most important book Bahá'u'lláh has given us, what would you say? (The answer is above).

DAY 9

A Prayer to Remember

Magnified be Thy Name, O God, Thou art the King, the Eternal Truth; Thou knowest what is in the heavens and on the earth …

Activity

Bahá'u'lláh wrote a book called the *Kitáb-i-Íqán*. This book gives us the overall plan of God for humankind. Shoghi Effendi, the Guardian of the Bahá'í Faith, informed us that next to the Kitáb-i-Aqdas, the *Kitáb-i-Íqán* is Bahá'u'lláh's most special book. Shoghi Effendi has said it tells us 'the Grand Redemptive Scheme of God'. I know that is very difficult to understand but it means the plan of God. Shoghi Effendi's words are very powerful so you should become familiar with them.

Bahá'ís are working on plans constantly. Find out what plan we are working on now.

For Consultation

Discuss the current plan plan together, briefly.

DAY 10

A Prayer to Remember

Try to memorize the whole prayer.

> Magnified be Thy Name, O God, Thou art the King, the Eternal Truth; Thou knowest what is in the heavens and on the earth, and unto Thee must all return.
>
> The Báb

Activity

The Universal House of Justice is the name for the highest body of the Bahá'ís of the world. The nine men are elected by the National Spiritual Assembly members who gather at the International Convention in Haifa once every five years. The Universal House of Justice members live in Haifa. The House of Justice gives an overall plan and from there the plans go out to the entire world!

For Consultation

Ask your teacher to explain to you the amount of work and years it took to bring us this far as a Faith. There have been so many courageous people involved but most importantly the Báb, Bahá'u'lláh, 'Abdu'l-Bahá, Shoghi Effendi and the Greatest Holy Leaf.

DAY 11

A Prayer to Remember

Recite the prayer of the Báb by heart.

Activity

A wonderful, precious name is Bahíyyih Khánum. Can you say that? She was the Greatest Holy Leaf, daughter of Bahá'u'lláh. 'Abdu'l-Bahá loved His sister so much that He wished to shield her from 'all these our earthly cares' and all hardship but during her entire life she suffered. Read this part of a letter which 'Abdu'l-Bahá wrote about Bahíyyih Khánum:

> I dare make no mention of the feelings which separation from her has aroused in my heart, for whatever I should attempt to express in writing will assuredly be effaced by the tears which such sentiments must bring to my eyes.

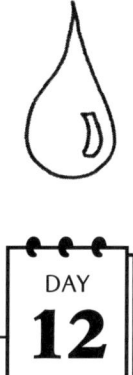

DAY 12

A Prayer to Remember

Say the whole prayer by heart.

Activity

When 'Abdu'l-Bahá passed on to the Abhá Kingdom in 1921, Bahíyyih Khánum comforted Shoghi Effendi and took the weight of the Faith on her shoulders until Shoghi Effendi could take on the Guardianship.

Find a photograph of the Greatest Holy Leaf. Try to read the story of Bahíyyih Khánum one day. You will feel great love for her for evermore.

For Consultation

Why do you think the loyal family of Bahá'u'lláh suffered so much in this world?

Day 13

A Prayer to Remember
Recite the prayer you have been memorizing today.

Activity
Some people have more than one name. Many of the stories of Bahá'í history are about people who are known by more than one name or title. For example, one of the first 18 people to find and recognize the Báb was a woman whose name was Fátimih-Umm Salamih. She was a 'Letter of the Living'. But you probably know her better as Ṭáhirih. Ṭáhirih is a title which means 'the Pure One'. She was also known as Qurratu'l-Ayn, which means 'the Solace of the Eyes', and also Zarrín-Táj, which means 'Crown of Gold'.

Do you know someone who is known by different names? Make a list of names of people who have two names, such as Robert and Bob, or Charlotte and Charlie. How many can you think of?

For Consultation
Why do some people have nicknames?

Day 14

A Prayer to Remember
Recite the prayer today.

Activity
Write in your dairy what you would like to do for the world!

For Consultation
People wish for fame so that they are known and respected by other people.

Remembering that God knows each of us and what is in our hearts, is it really necessary to seek fame?

A Prayer to Remember

Can you still say the whole prayer?

Activity

Humility is a radiant, shining quality. Look it up in the dictionary. Have you still got your string? Remember 'humility' today!

For Consultation

What causes people to boast and brag? What is behind it?

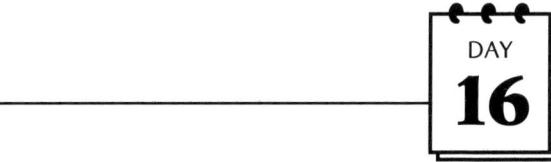

A Prayer to Remember

By now you will probably have no trouble in reciting the Báb's prayer by heart.

Activity

It might be very difficult but try now to draw or paint a picture of being humble, as you were all day yesterday. Did your parents notice last evening that you were wearing a string or did they notice a humble character?

For Consultation

Humility is not something you see easily. It might appear first as weakness or shyness or something quiet but actually it shines brightly and once you see it in a person, you will always admire it. Would you sincerely like to be humble?

DAY 17

A Prayer to Remember
Say the prayer of the Báb by heart.

Activity
Coming soon is the Feast of Might. Now that we have worked on the humble side of things, prepare to learn about 'might' and how humility and might work together.

Here is a situation: You are in class. The teacher is very excited and happy. He calls you up to the front of the room and he shouts with joy! 'Here is the best student in the school! His marks are the highest in the whole country and every university will be begging him to let them have the honour of inviting him to study there. Not only is this true but he is also the top sportsperson of the year and has won every trophy for the school possible. Have you heard him play the trumpet? He is like lightening! It is unbelievable to hear! How could he be all these things and also the most handsome boy in the school? We all love to look at him!'

Now suppose you were this boy (or, naturally, girl, if that is the case). How do you react to this dream come true? (Did I mention that you also have a spare million dollars?) Do you:

    a. Agree totally with every word and accept the applause of your fellow students.
    b. Appear overwhelmed and speechless except to remind your teacher that he forgot to mention the telegram from the queen.
    c. Become very confused and cry.
    d. Laugh with a spiteful glee, as you always knew you were the best and besides you don't even like these people.
    e. Thank the teacher politely and explain that it is all overrated and that your only wish in life is to be a worthy person.

For Consultation

Consult on what it means to have a good name or reputation.

A Prayer to Remember

Say the prayer of the Báb today from memory.

Activity

Practise saying the prayer you have learned in front of your teacher. It would be wonderful for you to say the prayer at the Feast.

For Consultation

When you attend a Nineteen Day Feast it refreshes and gladdens you. Can you discuss this with your teacher? Look forward to the Feast tomorrow.

A Prayer to Remember

Say the prayer of the Báb for the last time this month. Welcome all that you have learned and may it serve you well!

Activity

Write a story about a child named 'Wonderful'.

For Consultation

If you and your teacher could have any name of all the attributes of God, which ones would you choose? (Examples: Joy, Love, Justice, Might, Mercy, Perfection) Of course, this is just pretend but these are good things to wish for yourself!

10

Month of 'Izzat
(Might)

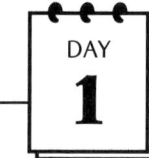
DAY 1

A Prayer to Remember

Say this prayer every day this month. By the end of the month you will know it by heart.

> O God, guide me, protect me, make of me a shining lamp and a brilliant star. Thou art the Mighty and the Powerful.
>
> *'Abdu'l-Bahá*

Activity

Write examples of things that you think are mighty.

For Consultation

Discuss these mighty things with your teacher.

DAY 2

A Prayer to Remember
Read the prayer for this month.

Activity
'Supreme power attributed to a divine Being' – this is what the dictionary says about the word 'might'. There is no end to the power of this kind of might. Any amount of power that humans can imagine comes nowhere near the might that God has. Think about this.

For Consultation
Do you feel that your teacher is 'mightier' than you? Why or why not?

DAY 3

A Prayer to Remember
Read the prayer for this month.

Activity
Try this exercise to learn about infinity. The reason why God is an unknown essence to us is that we are finite beings; that is, we have a beginning (conception) and an end (death of the body). God doesn't. God goes on and on and on and has always done so. Our soul goes on, back to God. This journey towards God is called eternal life.

∞

Take out your play dough and make little tiny balls. Make two balls out of one ball by pulling it in half. Take one of the smaller balls and do this again, no matter how small. If our fingers could do it, we could keep going and going. Count to the highest number you know and there will still be a higher number to climb to!

If you drew pencil marks on a paper you could keep going with more strokes even when the paper was so black you couldn't see them.

For Consultation

I used to wonder how it could be that there was always God. I thought He would have had to begin sometime. This is wrong. We live in a world of 'time' but God is independent of this world. Our world uses time but God's doesn't. Consult about this with your teacher.

DAY 4

A Prayer to Remember

See if you can say the prayer for this month by heart. Check to see if you are right.

Activity

Draw a picture of a clock. Draw a picture of the four seasons. We use time. We use minutes, hours and years.

For Consultation

We live for minutes, hours and years. We grow and we change. We change inside and outside. Discuss.

DAY 5

A Prayer to Remember

Recite the prayer you have learned for this month.

Activity

Draw a picture of an endless, windy road. If it goes out of sight, it doesn't mean it's finished. Draw a picture of the starry sky at night. Just because you see only so far and no farther, is that all there is? No! The sky goes on and on.

For Consultation

A clock is a part of our life to measure our time but it doesn't control the bigger side of our life which is endless and belongs to God. Do you understand this? This is a big idea to talk and talk about.

DAY 6

A Prayer to Remember

Recite the prayer you have learned for this month.

Activity

Compare the four pictures you drew in the past few days. All four pictures are a part of you! Draw one more picture – of your body and smiling face. Lie down and see if your teacher can trace you. The picture looks like you at this minute!

For Consultation

Think about the fact that your body is affected by the clock and seasons, that one day you will get old and will have lived a long time. The pictures of the sky and the winding road are like the things you have learned and received from God that go inside you. They don't end but they go free when God wishes to bring them nearer to His world. They want to go to Him – they go on and on. Only the body ends with the ticking away of time.

DAY 7

A Prayer to Remember

Recite the prayer you have learned for this month.

Activity

Hug yourself. You live in this wonderful body for now. Everyone has a body and a special 'light' inside that lives there. God keeps the light there.

For Consultation

When God wants a person to go home to Him, it happens. The body that the person lives in stops living. The 'light' that we are always close to, that part of us that always lives, is like a bird. Off it goes, free as a beautiful, flying bird, soaring closer to God! It is the happiest it has ever been! Our whole life in this world is a preparation for this new beginning! Talk about this.

DAY 8

A Prayer to Remember

Say the prayer for this month by heart.

Activity

Play-act: You are standing in a gateway near a river filled with gold and silver and a few snakes. You see your parents and your grandparents, whom you haven't seen for years and years, on the other side of the river. They are smiling and waving joyfully. You see a slender bridge over the water. What do you do?

For Consultation

Isn't it exciting to know that God says life goes on and that what we have learned is what we take with us? Discuss this.

DAY 9

A Prayer to Remember

Say the prayer for this month by heart.

Activity

The might of God never ends. We realize that through His might He can make anything He wants to happen become reality. He could make us rich. Be rich for a moment! RICH RICH RICH! Or He could make us rich and then we could lose it all. CRY CRY CRY! Act this out. Or He could give us the best friend in the world!! FRIEND FRIEND FRIEND! And He could teach us to love everyone! LOVE LOVE LOVE!

'Might' can be like a tiny seed which grows so well that it becomes very strong – like love!

DAY 10

A Prayer to Remember

Say the prayer for this month by heart.

Activity

Listen to some music that you both love!

For Consultation

When you love your parents, is it a mighty feeling?

DAY 11

A Prayer to Remember
Say the prayer for this month by heart.

Activity
Read a poem that you both love.

For Consultation
When you have a friend, is it a mighty feeling?

DAY 12

A Prayer to Remember
Say the prayer for this month by heart.

Activity
Read a story you both love.

For Consultation
When you read the prayer, did you love it? Did you feel it was your friend? Does the prayer have might?

Does mighty mean the biggest, most fearsome or does it mean the most wonderful, most lovely? Can mighty be a mighty lot of either or both of these things?

A Prayer to Remember

Say the prayer for this month by heart.

Activity

Every day your teacher takes time to be a mighty good friend to you. Time you said thank you!

For Consultation

When we say thank you to God in our prayers, we appreciate all the care He gives us. Consult on other ways we can thank God.

A Prayer to Remember

Say the prayer for this month by heart. You know it very well!

Activity

Your body is a good friend to you! Think about the different parts of your body, inside and out. If you can find a book about the body, you might like to read how the digestive system works.

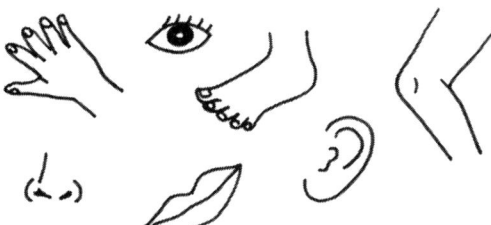

For Consultation
Is what you eat important to your body?

DAY 15

A Prayer to Remember
Say the prayer for this month by heart.

Activity
How do your muscles work? You should be able to find the answer in a book or encyclopedia.

For Consultation
Is exercise important to your body? Why?

DAY 16

A Prayer to Remember
Say the prayer for this month by heart.

Activity
Today think about your brain and how it functions. Read about this in your book.

For Consultation

Think with your brain about how important it is to think good thoughts about yourself and others. Is it something you think is important?

A Prayer to Remember

Say the prayer for this month by heart.

Activity

Today see if you can find out about your bones, what they are called and what they do in your body.

For Consultation

Isn't it amazing that a baby is born with its body all in place and ready to go! Some people have parts of their body that look different from others. Some people might think differently from us. But we are all the same in the eyes of God, aren't we?

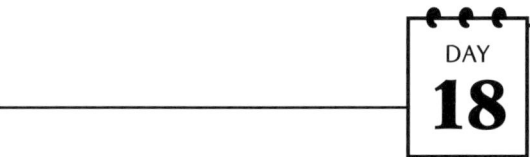

A Prayer to Remember

Say the prayer for this month by heart.

Activity

Today, see if you can find out about the largest organ in the body. Guess what it is? No ... no ... right! The SKIN!

Put a happy face on your skin. Did you feel the mouth move, the brain work, the muscles pull, a bone go up, your skin reposition?

For Consultation

How did all that happen?

A Prayer to Remember

Say the prayer for this month by heart. Well done!

Activity

Exercise your body. While you are at it, think a happy thought and smile!

For Consultation

I hope you enjoyed the Month of Might. You did very well! Now welcome to the Month of Will!

11

Month of Mashíyyat (Will)

DAY 1

A Reading to Remember

The beginning of all things is the knowledge of God, and the end of all things is strict observance of whatsoever hath been sent down from the empyrean of the Divine Will that pervadeth all that is in the heavens and all that is on the earth.

Bahá'u'lláh

During the month of Will (Mashíyyat) learn this verse of Bahá'u'lláh by heart. Practise saying it each day until you know it really well.

Activity

For your activity today, do whatever you want to do for a few minutes. Whatever you are allowed to do, that is!

For Consultation

Did you enjoy making the choice? How did it feel to decide and do what you like?

DAY 2

A Reading to Remember

Learn these words by heart:

> The beginning of all things is the knowledge of God …

Activity

For your activity today your teacher should tell you what to do. You should do it.

For Consultation

How does it feel to be told what to do? Is it different from deciding what to do for yourself? What is good about each of these?

DAY 3

A Reading to Remember

> The beginning of all things is the knowledge of God …

Activity

Walk into a wall. Pretend that you really want to get through but it is a wall and you have to stop.

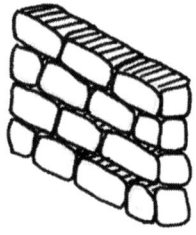

For Consultation

Imagine God is that wall. You have no power to get through the wall, so you stop. What do you think? Do you allow the wall to stop you or fight against the wall?

A Reading to Remember

The beginning of all things is the knowledge of God …

Activity

The reading for this month is very beautiful. To know God and to obey Him is our purpose in life. Write a story about a child who was given a precious gift. Write about his joy!

For Consultation

We have rules in life that we must follow. Pick out some of these and discuss them.

A Reading to Remember

Try to memorize a few more words of our passage:

> The beginning of all things is the knowledge of God, and the end of all things is strict observance …

Activity

Today write a story about a child who was given a broken toy with slime on it for his birthday. Write about his feelings.

For Consultation

Some rules are unpleasant but we must accept them. Talk about these.

A Reading to Remember

The beginning of all things is the knowledge of God, and the end of all things is strict observance ...

Activity

Today think about both stories you have written and prepare to write another one! Write about a child who was given a diamond ring and a huge bag of lollies but they were hidden inside a teddy bear with a monster head that had prickles all over the outside of it. Your job is to write a story that describes the feelings of the child and, if there is a moral to the story, what it is.

For Consultation

Ask you teacher to explain 'moral' to you.

DAY 7

A Reading to Remember

The beginning of all things is the knowledge of God, and the end of all things is strict observance …

Activity

Give yourself a gift: learn that God gives us gifts in different packages. Draw these ideas.

For Consultation

Are things always as they appear to be? Does God ask us to accept His will no matter how difficult it may be?

DAY 8

A Reading to Remember

Memorize a few more words of this verse:

> The beginning of all things is the knowledge of God, and the end of all things is strict observance of whatsoever hath been sent down from the empyrean of the Divine Will …

Activity

Remember when you were up against the wall and you couldn't go through? You realized that there was no way to get through and you had to find a new direction. Did the person who built your house expect you to go through a wall or walk down the hall to go from one room to the next? God gives us a path too. We have to find the way to stay on it. Take a fresh piece of paper and a pencil and design a house that you like. What does it need?

For Consultation

How does God show us His direction for us? Consult with your parents about how they find their direction.

DAY 9

A Reading to Remember

The beginning of all things is the knowledge of God, and the end of all things is strict observance of whatsoever hath been sent down from the empyrean of the Divine Will …

Activity

Do you have a dog? If so, you will know that when you care for him or command him to do something, it is all a part of your will. You desire him to sit, so you teach him. If he needs food, that is what you give him. Draw you and your pet or some other animal you know.

For Consultation

Does your pet always realize that what you are doing is best for him? Does he want to run in the street while you prefer that he be locked in the back yard?

DAY 10

A Reading to Remember

The beginning of all things is the knowledge of God, and the end of all things is strict observance of whatsoever hath been sent down from the empyrean of the Divine Will …

Activity

Ask your parents to arrange to have some family time tonight when they can talk with you about future plans for all of you. Perhaps now you can write down some things you would like to ask them.

For Reflection

We have free will to live our life and make our own choices. How do we do this if God's will is otherwise? Do we happily change our plans?

A Reading to Remember

Try to memorize a few more words of the passage:

> The beginning of all things is the knowledge of God, and the end of all things is strict observance of whatsoever hath been sent down from the empyrean of the Divine Will that pervadeth all that is in the heavens …

Activity

Is your room really tidy? Take some time now to set up an interesting looking table of your favourite things and straighten up your room.

For Consultation

Consult on being orderly in your life. Is it worthwhile?

DAY 12

A Reading to Remember

The beginning of all things is the knowledge of God, and the end of all things is strict observance of whatsoever hath been sent down from the empyrean of the Divine Will that pervadeth all that is in the heavens …

Activity

Write a letter to your pen pal and tell him or her what you put on your table yesterday. Make your letter interesting and it will tell your pen pal a lot about you. You can ask him whether he likes any of those things too!

For Reflection

Does everyone wake up in the morning and eat breakfast, wash, dress and go to school, work or play? Do many people pray every morning? Do you?

DAY 13

A Reading to Remember

The beginning of all things is the knowledge of God, and the end of all things is strict observance of whatsoever hath been sent down from the empyrean of the Divine Will that pervadeth all that is in the heavens …

For Reflection

Have you learned this reading by heart yet? Maybe you would like to say it at the Feast of Knowledge, which is a few days away. It is such an interesting reading, isn't it?

Does your teacher at school know you are trying to learn these things every day?

DAY 14

A Reading to Remember

Now try memorizing the last few words. If you do, you will know the whole verse!

> The beginning of all things is the knowledge of God, and the end of all things is strict observance of whatsoever hath been sent down from the empyrean of the Divine Will that pervadeth all that is in the heavens and all that is on the earth.
>
> *Bahá'u'lláh*

Activity

Water the plants for your mother. (Unless they shouldn't be watered!) Ask her if she would like to plant any seeds. It is good to care for things and watch them grow.

For Reflection

Bahá'u'lláh taught us the will of God. Everything He did was the will of God. This is why when we pray to God through Bahá'u'lláh we obey God. He sent Bahá'u'lláh to us and we obey Him.

A Reading to Remember

See if you can say the whole verse without looking.

Activity

Whether we love our life or whether we don't is really up to us. It is our 'free will'. We make our choices. If we were unjustly thrown into prison we could still choose to be happy and abide by the will of God. Many Bahá'ís have been imprisoned for believing in Bahá'u'lláh but they have been happy. Let's have a moment of silence to show respect for those who have given us such an example.

For Consultation

Life is often hard. What is the hardest thing for you to do at the present time?

A Reading to Remember

Say the verse of Bahá'u'lláh by heart.

Activity

Do you have a hobby or craft that you would like to do now? Maybe your teacher could have a look at what you're doing.

For Consultation
Have a chat about the craft you have chosen to do.

A Reading to Remember
Say the verse of Bahá'u'lláh again by heart.

Activity
If you were in danger because someone was doing something dangerous and involving you, what would the wise thing be to do? Practise a situation like this with your teacher. This is also a part of your free will. Should you go along with someone who is endangering you?

For Consultation
Life is very special and we have to protect it. Consult on being safe and sensible. Consult about what friends do that affects them badly and talk about how to use your common sense if you are afraid of a situation.

A Reading to Remember
Can you remember all the words of the verse you have been learning? Say it once again.

Activity
There is only one you. You think your own way, your heart is your own and your lovely little smile is your own and very important to the world. Be yourself! Write down in your diary a promise to take care of yourself because we need you!

For Consultation

We are all one family and we pray for the security of this world, which can only come from seeing ourselves as brothers and sisters. What can you do to help people get together? You could offer your suggestion at the Nineteen Day Feast. It may help your community think of a way to teach others about the Faith.

A Reading to Remember

Say the whole verse of Bahá'u'lláh by heart.

Activity

Make a plate of food that you can take to the Feast. Your parents can help you decide what to make.

For Reflection

You have been a very interesting student. Thank you for learning so much in the month of Will.

12

Month of 'Ilm
(Knowledge)

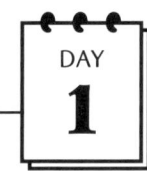
DAY 1

A Reading to Remember

O thou verdant plant of the Abhá Paradise! O thou tender sapling of the rose garden of immortality!

Although thou art but a tiny creature in this world of existence, yet it is my earnest hope that thou wilt become great in the kingdom of heaven. Although a mere child, yet praise be to God that through the strengthening power of faith and certitude thou art indeed as a grown-up and mature soul. Know thou of a certainty that those of tender age in the Abhá Garden shall inherit the realm of the kingdom and that the outpourings of celestial grace encompass the children in the school of the love of God. It is my hope that through the manifold bounties of Him Who is the Lord of Oneness thou mayest be reared and nurtured beside this heavenly stream which floweth in the rose garden of divine guidance.

Upon thee be the glory of the Most Glorious.

'Abdu'l-Bahá

This is one of the most beautiful of the children's readings. If you read this faithfully you will have much guidance for the rest of your life!

Activity

One dictionary meaning of knowledge is 'the state or fact of knowing – familiarity, awareness or understanding gained through experience or study – that which is known'. Look up 'knowledge' in the dictionary and see all of the meanings. It is good for you to learn all the different meanings of words to develop your vocabulary!

For Consultation

Knowledge is a subject that comes to us through all the doors of life. How do you think we obtain knowledge?

DAY 2

A Reading to Remember

Learn this portion of the reading by heart:

> O thou verdant plant of the Abhá Paradise! O thou tender sapling of the rose garden of immortality!

Activity

Make a chart and label it KNOWLEDGE. Design it any way you like, in consultation with your teacher. The purpose of the chart is to realize that we receive knowledge from many sources. Some things we learn in more than one way but knowledge does relate subjects to each other. If you learn to bake a cake you have also learned about how an oven works, how milk splashes, what fun it is to lick a bowl – those are just the obvious things. You could say you also learned how matter changes from one state (semi-liquid) to another (solid). It is up to you to think about how much you learn and where to put it on the chart. Keep the chart daily for one week and you will be surprised!

DAY 3

A Reading to Remember

Learn this portion of the reading by heart:

> O thou verdant plant of the Abhá Paradise! O thou tender sapling of the rose garden of immortality!
>
> Although thou art but a tiny creature in this world of existence, yet it is my earnest hope that thou wilt become great in the kingdom of heaven.

Activity

Put something down on your chart that you have learned today. Did you

    a. read anything
    b. telephone a friend
    c. go to school
    d. do something else?

For Consultation

For your consultation consider the subjects you learn in school. Think about what you learn in sports, crafts, music or the arts. Consider what you learn in your Bahá'í children's class. Consult about what you learn from other people. Is there any place else you learn?

A Reading to Remember

Memorize the reading up to here.

> O thou verdant plant of the Abhá Paradise! O thou tender sapling of the rose garden of immortality!
>
> Although thou art but a tiny creature in this world of existence, yet it is my earnest hope that thou wilt become great in the kingdom of heaven. Although a mere child, yet praise be to God that through the strengthening power of faith and certitude thou art indeed as a grown-up and mature soul.

For Consultation

With your teacher, begin to discuss the meanings of the words and phrases in the reading by 'Abdu'l-Bahá.

A Reading to Remember

A few more words to memorize:

> O thou verdant plant of the Abhá Paradise! O thou tender sapling of the rose garden of immortality!
>
> Although thou art but a tiny creature in this world of existence,

yet it is my earnest hope that thou wilt become great in the kingdom of heaven. Although a mere child, yet praise be to God that through the strengthening power of faith and certitude thou art indeed as a grown-up and mature soul. Know thou of a certainty that those of tender age in the Abhá Garden shall inherit the realm of the kingdom …

Activity

Today put another bit of learning on your chart of knowledge. This is unique to you. Please don't hesitate to write down what you think you have learned in an experience you had yesterday or today.

For Consultation

Talk about what you learned with your teacher and all the different facts (sides) of it. Your teacher can help you get the most out of what you know!

DAY 6

A Reading to Remember

Learn more of this reading by heart:

> O thou verdant plant of the Abhá Paradise! O thou tender sapling of the rose garden of immortality!
>
> Although thou art but a tiny creature in this world of existence, yet it is my earnest hope that thou wilt become great in the kingdom of heaven. Although a mere child, yet praise be to God that through the strengthening power of faith and certitude thou art indeed as a grown-up and mature soul. Know thou of a certainty that those of tender age in the Abhá Garden shall inherit the realm of the kingdom and that the outpourings of celestial grace encompass the children in the school of the love of God.

For Consultation

With your teacher, continue to discuss the meanings of the words and phrases in this reading.

DAY 7

A Reading to Remember

> O thou verdant plant of the Abhá Paradise! O thou tender sapling of the rose garden of immortality!
>
> Although thou art but a tiny creature in this world of existence, yet it is my earnest hope that thou wilt become great in the kingdom of heaven. Although a mere child, yet praise be to God that through the strengthening power of faith and certitude thou art indeed as a grown-up and mature soul. Know thou of a certainty that those of tender age in the Abhá Garden shall inherit the realm of the kingdom and that the outpourings of celestial grace encompass the children in the school of the love of God. It is my hope that through the manifold bounties of Him Who is the Lord of Oneness …

Activity

Again put some knowledge on your chart!

For Consultation

What is the purpose of going to school? Stop and think about it, then consult on the purpose of school.

DAY 8

A Reading to Remember

You know almost the whole reading now – keep going!

> O thou verdant plant of the Abhá Paradise! O thou tender sapling of the rose garden of immortality!
>
> Although thou art but a tiny creature in this world of existence,

yet it is my earnest hope that thou wilt become great in the kingdom of heaven. Although a mere child, yet praise be to God that through the strengthening power of faith and certitude thou art indeed as a grown-up and mature soul. Know thou of a certainty that those of tender age in the Abhá Garden shall inherit the realm of the kingdom and that the outpourings of celestial grace encompass the children in the school of the love of God. It is my hope that through the manifold bounties of Him Who is the Lord of Oneness thou mayest be reared and nurtured beside this heavenly stream which floweth in the rose garden of divine guidance.

Activity

There have been many, many wise Bahá'í scholars. Each in his own way has taught the Faith with excellence. How do you teach the Faith? Teach your teacher something about the Bahá'í Faith.

For Consultation

So, you have been teaching the Faith in your own way! Very good! What does your teacher say she has learned?

DAY 9

A Reading to Remember

O thou verdant plant of the Abhá Paradise! O thou tender sapling of the rose garden of immortality!

Although thou art but a tiny creature in this world of existence, yet it is my earnest hope that thou wilt become great in the kingdom of heaven. Although a mere child, yet praise be to God that through the strengthening power of faith and certitude thou art indeed as a grown-up and mature soul. Know thou of a certainty that those of tender age in the Abhá Garden shall inherit the realm of the kingdom and that the outpourings of celestial grace encompass the children in the school of the love of God. It is my hope that through the manifold bounties of Him Who is the Lord of Oneness thou mayest be reared and nurtured beside this heavenly stream which floweth in the rose garden of divine guidance.

Upon thee be the glory of the Most Glorious.

'Abdu'l-Bahá

Now you know the whole prayer by heart! Don't worry if you haven't perfected it yet. You'll have the opportunity to do so later in the month.

A Reading to Remember

Try to learn this Hidden Word by heart.

> O Son of Spirit! The best beloved of all things in My sight is Justice; turn not away therefrom if thou desirest Me, and neglect it not that I may confide in thee. By its aid thou shalt see with thine own eyes and not through the eyes of others, and shalt know of thine own knowledge and not through the knowledge of thy neighbour. Ponder this in thy heart; how it behoveth thee to be. Verily justice is My gift to thee and the sign of My loving-kindness. Set it then before thine eyes.

Bahá'u'lláh

Activity

If two people read the same sentence, they are very likely to get two entirely different meanings from it.

It's no wonder there are arguments all over the place! How do we prevent an argument? We state our opinions in an open discussion and we listen to each other and explain how we feel. The two people may decide not to agree but each has had a chance to speak and be heard. Practise this. Can you find a way of feeling comfortable with the other person?

For Consultation

What did you learn from the activity? Put it on your chart.

A Reading to Remember

Memorize this part of the Hidden Word.

> O Son of Spirit! The best beloved of all things in My sight is Justice; turn not away therefrom if thou desirest Me, and neglect it not that I may confide in thee.

Activity

Take a look at the food you eat. Your mother and father may well cook what their parents cooked and they cooked what their parents cooked and so on back into time. People often cook what their parents taught them to eat. This is traditional learning. We didn't decide to eat certain foods cooked and certain ones raw. We really learned this as we grew up. Knowledge can be traditional and this has a very big influence on our lives. Think about and chart some of the traditional knowledge you have.

For Consultation

Does knowledge change? Scientists and inventors change the scope of what humankind knows. They experiment with knowledge until something remarkable happens and they can take us a step further in our understanding. This is actually knowledge which is given to us from God even though we usually call it science!

One of the Bahá'í principles is that science and religion are in harmony. Consult on why this is true.

DAY 12

A Reading to Remember

Try to memorize more of this Hidden Word.

> O Son of Spirit! The best beloved of all things in My sight is Justice; turn not away therefrom if thou desirest Me, and neglect it not that I may confide in thee. By its aid thou shalt see with thine own eyes and not through the eyes of others, and shalt know of thine own knowledge and not through the knowledge of thy neighbour.

Activity

Prejudice is not advantageous to anyone and must be eliminated from our lives. This is a Bahá'í principle for our social development. You be blue and have your teacher be yellow. Work out how it feels to be blue when the rest of the world is red. Work out a solution to your problem and present it to the United Nations General Assembly!

For Consultation

Prejudice cannot be justified as humanity was created by the one God. When you see any sort of prejudice, recognize it and stay away from it. Imagine children at your school teasing a very tubby girl. Is this fair?

A Reading to Remember

Learn a little more of this Hidden Word.

> O Son of Spirit! The best beloved of all things in My sight is Justice; turn not away therefrom if thou desirest Me, and neglect it not that I may confide in thee. By its aid thou shalt see with thine own eyes and not through the eyes of others, and shalt know of thine own knowledge and not through the knowledge of thy neighbour. Ponder this in thy heart; how it behoveth thee to be.

Activity

Before we can understand some things in life we need to experience them. If you have a visually impaired child in your family you understand how to cope with the situation. You love your sister and you help her do the things she might not be able to do on her own or you assist her as she does things her way. You know how your parents have learned to adjust their lives as well. Your sister, like you, probably has begun to learn new things. You also realize some things that others do not – how important touch is, how useful hands and ears are, and countless other things you and your family have learned through the special needs of your sister and your family.

For Consultation

Let's answer some questions.

- In the situation described above, how important is patience?
- Does everyone you meet have patience?
- Are people outside of the family aware of all the things you know about being visually impaired?
- Do people who don't see have lots of special talents? What are they?
- What forms of prejudice exist that make being visually impaired harder?
- What examples can you give of people being prejudiced against each other?
- What is your opinion of prejudice and why?

DAY 14

A Reading to Remember

Add a few more words to your Hidden Word.

> O Son of Spirit! The best beloved of all things in My sight is Justice; turn not away therefrom if thou desirest Me, and neglect it not that I may confide in thee. By its aid thou shalt see with thine own eyes and not through the eyes of others, and shalt know of thine own knowledge and not through the knowledge of thy neighbour. Ponder this in thy heart; how it behoveth thee to be. Verily justice is My gift to thee and the sign of My loving-kindness.

Activity

Sometimes we refer to someone who does not accept knowledge as being blind. This statement has nothing to do with a person's eyes. It has to do with his heart or his state of mind.

Draw a picture of a pair of eyes. Make it quite big so you can write some words in the iris (coloured part of the eyeball). Write down what you see if you 'see with knowledge'.

DAY 15

A Reading to Remember

O Son of Spirit! The best beloved of all things in My sight is Justice; turn not away therefrom if thou desirest Me, and neglect it not that I may confide in thee. By its aid thou shalt see with thine own eyes and not through the eyes of others, and shalt know of thine own knowledge and not through the knowledge of thy neighbour. Ponder this in thy heart; how it behoveth thee to be. Verily justice is My gift to thee and the sign of My loving-kindness. Set it then before thine eyes.

Bahá'u'lláh

Congratulations! You now know another of the sacred writings.

Activity

Make a mobile. One idea is to draw and cut out many different eyes. When hung as a mobile they would each look different and remind you of all the different points of view each eye would see. Design a mobile of your own creation now.

For Consultation

What one thing that you know is dearer to you than any other thing in the world? Discuss this with your teacher or parent.

DAY 16

A Reading to Remember

Do you recall this reading? Perhaps you know it by heart or maybe there are still some sections that you are unsure of. See how well you can learn 'Abdu'l-Bahá's words during the remaining days of this month.

> O thou verdant plant of the Abhá Paradise! O thou tender sapling of the rose garden of immortality!
>
> Although thou art but a tiny creature in this world of existence, yet it is my earnest hope that thou wilt become great in the kingdom of heaven. Although a mere child, yet praise be to God that through the strengthening power of faith and certitude thou art indeed as a grown-up and mature soul. Know thou of a certainty that those of tender age in the Abhá Garden shall inherit the realm of the kingdom and that the outpourings of celestial grace encompass the children in the school of the love of God. It is my hope that through the manifold bounties of Him Who is the Lord of Oneness thou mayest be reared and nurtured beside this heavenly stream which floweth in the rose garden of divine guidance.
>
> Upon thee be the glory of the Most Glorious.
>
> *'Abdu'l-Bahá*

Activity

If you have more work to do on the mobile, such as cutting out what you drew or designing the way to hang it, use a few minutes now.

For Consultation

Ask your teacher if he knows everything. If he says no, ask him what he doesn't know. This could take quite a while. If he says he knows everything, you need a new teacher!

DAY 17

A Reading to Remember

Say the same reading you said yesterday.

Activity

I hope that you have managed to hang your mobile and that you like it. You can always experiment, change it or make another one ... or many! The important thing about becoming knowledgeable is that it goes on and on. For your activity today, you choose what you would like to do. Make sure you will learn something.

For Consultation

Bahá'ís try to be a good example so that they can give the knowledge they have to other people. If you love someone, by loving him you are teaching him to love others. If you show patience, the chances are another person will not only notice but try as well. What happens when people say that others should be loving but don't show it themselves? What happens when people say others should be patient but forget to be patient themselves? Think of other examples of behaviour.

DAY 18

A Reading to Remember

Say the same reading you said yesterday – from memory, if you can.

Activity

Write a short poem about knowledge. Try to make the verses rhyme with these words: know, grow, show.

For Consultation

Read your poem to your teacher. Would you like to share it at the Feast?

A Reading to Remember

Say the same reading you said yesterday.

Activity

If you read every book in the world's biggest library, you would get a tremendous amount of knowledge. But to know about Bahá'u'lláh is by far the most complete knowledge in this world. Do you realize how wonderful it is to be learning about being a Bahá'í? Write in your diary what you know about Bahá'u'lláh and being one of His followers.

For Consultation

Ask your teacher how he became a Bahá'í. Ask him what he has learned.

13

Month of Qudrat
(Power)

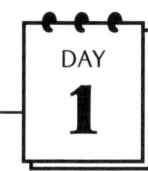

A Prayer to Remember

This prayer by Bahá'u'lláh is a prayer for journeys. Try to read it today. The word 'contumacious' means 'disobedient'.

> O God, my God! I have set out from my home, holding fast unto the cord of Thy love, and I have committed myself wholly to Thy care and Thy protection. I entreat Thee by Thy power through which Thou didst protect Thy loved ones from the wayward and the perverse, and from every contumacious oppressor, and every wicked doer who hath strayed far from Thee, to keep me safe by Thy bounty and Thy grace. Enable me, then, to return to my home by Thy power and Thy might. Thou art, truly, the Almighty, the Help in Peril, the Self-Subsisting.
>
> *Bahá'u'lláh*

Activity

Today would be a good time to write to your pen pal. If you wish to write to someone else for a change, that would be a good thing to do. Everyone loves to get a letter. Why not write to your grandparents, an old friend who has moved away (if you have one!) or a friend who would be surprised to get a letter? If they are Bahá'ís, perhaps you could ask them what they think about the Bahá'í month of Power. They might introduce a few thoughts to you, just as we try to do in your class here! In any case, writing a letter shares a lot of fun.

For Consultation

One definition of the word 'power' is 'the ability to do or act'. Another is 'influential person' and another is 'mechanical energy as opposed to hand labour'. Still another definition is 'Deity (God)'. Think of examples of power that come under these definitions.

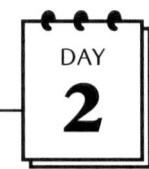

DAY 2

A Prayer to Remember

Learn this portion of the prayer by heart.

> O God, my God! I have set out from my home, holding fast unto the cord of Thy love …

Activity

List, draw or explain all the things you can think of that show power.

For Consultation

Discuss these with your teacher. Tell her why you think power exists in each.

A Prayer to Remember

Memorize the prayer up to here.

> O God, my God! I have set out from my home, holding fast unto the cord of Thy love, and I have committed myself wholly to Thy care and Thy protection.

Activity

Act out the following powerful things:

Car	Pulley	Eagle
Sun	TV	Wind
Teacher	Parents	Government
	Rocket ship	

For Consultation

Consult with your teacher. Can simple things like books or leaves or furniture have power?

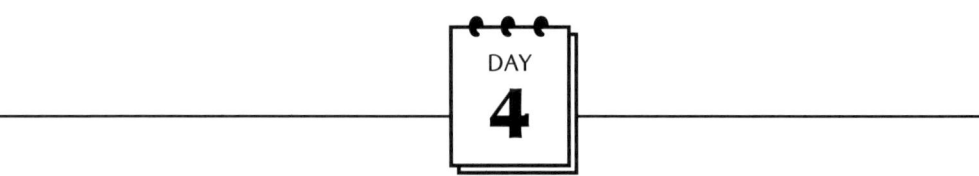

A Prayer to Remember

More of the prayer to learn.

> O God, my God! I have set out from my home, holding fast unto the cord of Thy love, and I have committed myself wholly to Thy care and Thy protection. I entreat Thee by Thy power through which Thou didst protect Thy loved ones from the wayward and the perverse …

Activity

Draw a picture of the power in the prayer you just said. Does God help us do things like return home? Does God protect us through His power? Try to put this in a picture. Your teacher might help you decide on where to start.

For Consultation

Is there power in certain words? Is there power in words from God? Is there power in the prayer you are learning?

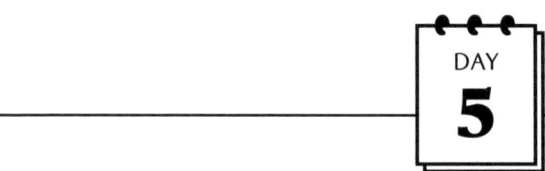

A Prayer to Remember

Add more to the prayer.

> O God, my God! I have set out from my home, holding fast unto the cord of Thy love, and I have committed myself wholly to Thy

care and Thy protection. I entreat Thee by Thy power through which Thou didst protect Thy loved ones from the wayward and the perverse, and from every contumacious oppressor, and every wicked doer who hath strayed far from Thee …

Activity

Find one book in your Bahá'í library at home which has a short story in it. Read it and retell it to your teacher.

For Consultation

Did your teacher enjoy your story? Do you know this story now and will you remember it? Will you be able to tell it again sometime?

DAY 6

A Prayer to Remember

You have learned nearly the whole prayer.

> O God, my God! I have set out from my home, holding fast unto the cord of Thy love, and I have committed myself wholly to Thy care and Thy protection. I entreat Thee by Thy power through which Thou didst protect Thy loved ones from the wayward and the perverse, and from every contumacious oppressor, and every wicked doer who hath strayed far from Thee, to keep me safe by Thy bounty and Thy grace.

Activity

Take some play dough and build something. Notice how the heaviest part of the dough is usually at the bottom of what you built. The bottom of your building takes the weight of what is above. Experiment with this.

For Consultation

Much of humankind is ruled by a power, a government leader such as a prime minister or a president. In some countries, one person may make many of the final decisions about how we live. In the Bahá'í Faith decisions are made by a group of people who talk together first. Each person has a chance to speak, just as you and your teacher do. At the local level, decisions are made by the Local Spiritual Assembly. At the national level it is the National Spiritual Assembly that decides. The Universal House of Justice makes decisions for the whole world. Bahá'ís elect their Local Assembly and elect delegates who elect the National Spiritual Assembly. The National Assembly members elect the Universal House of Justice. In this way, every individual has a chance to have his ideas consulted upon. Decisions couldn't be made more fairly than this. What do you think about power being fair?

DAY 7

A Prayer to Remember

O God, my God! I have set out from my home, holding fast unto the cord of Thy love, and I have committed myself wholly to Thy care and Thy protection. I entreat Thee by Thy power through which Thou didst protect Thy loved ones from the wayward and the perverse, and from every contumacious oppressor, and every wicked doer who hath strayed far from Thee, to keep me safe by Thy bounty and Thy grace. Enable me, then, to return to my home by Thy power and Thy might.

Just a few more words to learn!

Activity

Cut out lots of pictures of people from magazines. Throw them up in the air and then put them in piles of nine at random. These could be nine people on an Assembly! Glue them together on strips of paper. Save them until tomorrow.

Sing a song with your teacher. 'Look at me, follow me, be as I am. 'Abdu'l-Bahá' is a beautiful song.

A Prayer to Remember

O God, my God! I have set out from my home, holding fast unto the cord of Thy love, and I have committed myself wholly to Thy care and Thy protection. I entreat Thee by Thy power through which Thou didst protect Thy loved ones from the wayward and the perverse, and from every contumacious oppressor, and every wicked doer who hath strayed far from Thee, to keep me safe by Thy bounty and Thy grace. Enable me, then, to return to my home by Thy power and Thy might. Thou art, truly, the Almighty, the Help in Peril, the Self-Subsisting.

Bahá'u'lláh

Now you know the whole prayer.

Activity

Take your strips of people and begin to make a ladder. The people can be the rungs and the sides of the ladder can be made with any material you have. At the top of the ladder glue a prayer for humanity. Think of jobs that each group of nine could do to help humankind. You could glue your own picture in one of the groups and write what you feel about the work your Assembly does. Anything you or your teacher can think of that has to do with the power of working in a group would be interesting. You could perhaps take your picture ladder and your list of ideas to a Nineteen Day Feast and let the adults know what you think.

For Consultation

What does power mean to you?

DAY 9

A Prayer to Remember

See if you can say the whole prayer you have learned by heart.

Activity

Do a power dance! Use your imagination! If you have some music that is suitable, you could dance to it.

For Consultation

Do you go all silly when you do a power dance or do you show strength? Do you make powerful patterns or what?

DAY 10

A Reading to Remember

In this quotation Bahá'u'lláh talks about the power of God's name and asks us if we are prepared to give up the 'things that men possess' for the things that God wants us to have. Over the coming days, learn this passage by heart by remembering a small section each day.

> Who is there among you, O people, who will renounce the world, and draw nigh unto God, the Lord of all names? Where is he to be found who, through the power of My name that transcendeth all created things, will cast away the things that men possess, and cling, with all his might to the things which God, the Knower of the unseen and of the seen, hath bidden him observe?
>
> *Bahá'u'lláh*

Activity

Ask permission to take some saucepans and a lid and spoon from the kitchen. Get ready for some powerful music! Set it up and go. Now stop! Does the music have to be loud and banging? Could it have a soft pattern that also sounds powerful? Could it have a rhythm that sounds like a motor running or water flowing or a horse galloping? Invent some powerful patterns of music.

For Consultation

What is more powerful to you of these two things: A prayer or an army tank? A song of peace or a million dollars? A happy family or 25 fighting soldiers?

DAY 11

A Reading to Remember

Learn this section of Bahá'u'lláh's writings by heart.

> Who is there amongst you, O people, who will renounce the world …

Activity

Invent a machine that could keep the world running in perfect order. Draw it or speak about it and list the things it needs to be able to do.

For Consultation

What else do we know of that can keep the world running in perfect order? Is the answer God?

DAY 12

A Reading to Remember

Learn this section of the passage by heart.

> Who is there among you, O people, who will renounce the world, and draw nigh unto God, the Lord of all names?

Activity

Look back to the month of Raḥmat and read once again the story of the bundle of sticks on Day 8 of that month.

For Consultation

What was this story all about?

DAY 13

A Reading to Remember

Add a few more words to the verse of Bahá'u'lláh:

> Who is there among you, O people, who will renounce the world, and draw nigh unto God, the Lord of all names? Where is he to be found who, through the power of My name that transcendeth all created things …

Activity

Love is a power tool. When you love somebody you have a special feeling that creates very good things. You are happy and you like doing things for that person. Go and pick some flowers for your family, or if you can't do that, think of another little expression of love that you can make now.

For Consultation

Whom do you love? Do you love everybody as God wants us to do?

A Reading to Remember

Who is there among you, O people, who will renounce the world, and draw nigh unto God, the Lord of all names? Where is he to be found who, through the power of My name that transcendeth all created things, will cast away the things that men possess …

Activity

Today make a plan to make everyone happy. No matter how careful you have to be, think very positively that you can have a special day of sharing love and happiness with everyone.

For Consultation

Does God love us? Does He show us love even if we don't see it? Can you talk about this?

A Reading to Remember

Now say the entire passage.

Who is there among you, O people, who will renounce the world, and draw nigh unto God, the Lord of all names? Where is he to be found who, through the power of My name that transcendeth all created things, will cast away the things that men possess, and cling, with all his might to the things which God, the Knower of the unseen and of the seen, hath bidden him observe?

Bahá'u'lláh

Activity

Pretend you are the editor of the local paper. What would the headlines say if suddenly all the power in the world were used for the good of humankind? Take a sheet of paper and make some NEWS! You will need to write headlines and a cover story. Then mark out enough columns to write more stories about this tomorrow.

For Consultation

When you state your opinion, you have a lot of 'power'. You can say things that are good or bad. What do you think about the power you have to speak your mind?

DAY 16

A Reading to Remember

Say the passage from Bahá'u'lláh's writings that you said yesterday. Can you say any of it by heart?

Activity

Back to the drawing board. Write another story on the front page about yourself doing things that are powerful and good.

For Consultation

Read this story to your teacher and she can help you make it sound like a news story.

A Reading to Remember

Recite the passage you said yesterday.

Activity

Now pretend you are the reporter and your teacher is a Bahá'í scientist. Ask her the questions that explain how this power for good works. Take notes and then tomorrow you can write it in story form. Draw how she looks so that you have a photograph for your story.

At the Feast of Qawl (Speech) in a couple of days you could interview your teacher (or a stand-in) for a bit of entertainment in the social portion. If you like this idea, practise it now.

A Prayer to Remember

How well have you remembered this prayer?

> O God, my God! I have set out from my home, holding fast unto the cord of Thy love, and I have committed myself wholly to Thy care and Thy protection. I entreat Thee by Thy power through which Thou didst protect Thy loved ones from the wayward and the perverse, and from every contumacious oppressor, and every wicked doer who hath strayed far from Thee, to keep me safe by Thy bounty and Thy grace. Enable me, then, to return to my home by Thy power and Thy might. Thou art, truly, the Almighty, the Help in Peril, the Self-Subsisting.
>
> *Bahá'u'lláh*

Activity

Remember the reporting you did yesterday. Write out your story and paste on your picture. If there is still room on the front page, make some ads for your paper or put in a weather report or whatever you think will express this new world of good power. Have fun! Show your teacher what a good newspaper is.

DAY 19

A Prayer to Remember

Practise saying by heart the prayer you said yesterday one last time.

Activity

When your newspaper is finished you can put contact paper on it or hang it with a picture hook. You have worked hard on it and one day you will be thrilled to see it, so save it.

For Consultation

People definitely like good news. It spreads goodwill and the power of love. The Nineteen Day Feast is a blessed occasion to share this warmth. Consult on how you enter the Nineteen Day Feast.

14

Month of Qawl (Speech)

DAY 1

A Reading to Remember

Learn this Hidden Word of Bahá'u'lláh during this Bahá'í month.

> O Companion of My Throne! Hear no evil, and see no evil, abase not thyself, neither sigh nor weep. Speak no evil, that thou mayest not hear it spoken unto thee, and magnify not the faults of others that thine own faults may not appear great; and wish not the abasement of anyone, that thine own abasement be not exposed. Live then the days of thy life, that are less than a fleeting moment, with thy mind stainless, thy heart unsullied, thy thoughts pure, and thy nature sanctified, so that, free and content, thou mayest put away this mortal frame, and repair unto the mystic paradise and abide in the eternal kingdom for evermore.
>
> *Bahá'u'lláh*

Activity

Here is the dictionary meaning of 'speech': 1. The act of speaking; 2. That which is spoken; 3. The language of a nation. When you talk, this is speech. What you say, that is, your words, are called speech. The language you speak is speech. For this month let's think of a subject, write a speech and give a speech in 19 days! Some of the most wonderful speakers in the world just happen to have been Bahá'ís. You could be one of them. Get a subject in mind now. If you are very young, your teacher can help you decide.

For Consultation

Talk about your subject with your teacher and think of a few things you would like to say about your subject.

A Reading to Remember

Learn this portion of the Hidden Word today.

    O Companion of My Throne!

Activity

Get a note pad and write down interesting points you will put into your speech. Label them with numbers so that they go in an order. Order is very important in a speech. People can follow what you are saying if it is in order.

For Consultation

Now stop what you are doing and consult on this. How do speech and consultation go together? Does this have anything to do with speaking and listening?

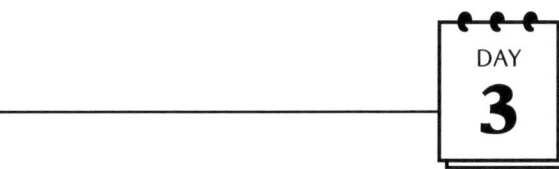

A Reading to Remember

O Companion of My Throne! Hear no evil, and see no evil …

Activity

Ask your teacher to help you finalize the order in which your points will sound the best. Make sure you begin the speech by explaining your intention or with an interesting, funny or clever sentence or two to gain the listener's attention. The ending is also very important. It needs to sum up what you said or be interesting in some special way.

For Consultation

Discuss this while you work and share ideas.

A Reading to Remember

O Companion of My Throne! Hear no evil, and see no evil, abase not thyself …

For Consultation

Once there was a Bahá'í named Martha Root. She travelled around the world four times and visited many countries. In each place she spoke of the Faith, broadcast information about it or translated Bahá'í material into the local language. She used every possible situation to speak of the Faith. And her speeches were very, very good! Sometimes she spoke to kings and queens and very famous people; sometimes she spoke to whoever she was with. Books and stories have been written about Martha Root. When you are older I hope you be able to read some of these. Martha Root was a great speaker.

Martha Root's speeches were full of Bahá'í love. She wanted to give this precious gift to everyone. This love wasn't said in her words. It was given from her heart while she spoke. Discuss this with your teacher. What would you like to give your listeners in the speech you are writing? Tomorrow your teacher can read for you the beginning of one of Martha Root's most loving messages!

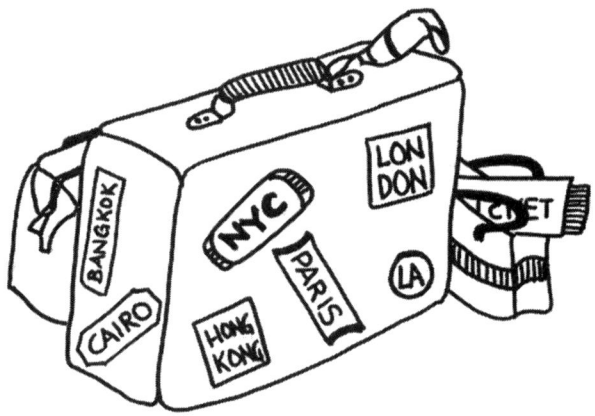

DAY 5

A Reading to Remember

O Companion of My Throne! Hear no evil, and see no evil, abase not thyself, neither sigh nor weep.

Activity

Take your notes now and see whether they are in outline form. Have you labelled the different thoughts? Next to the first one write a sentence of what you are going to say. Go to point two and again write a sentence about that thought. Continue with this for a few minutes. You can make changes later, so don't be worried about how it sounds.

Now relax and let your teacher read you the work of an expert, Martha Root:

> I am happy to speak to you this evening about one of the greatest young women in the world, one of the most spiritual, one of the greatest poets of Írán, and the first woman of her time in Central Asia to lay aside the veil and work for the equal education of the girl and the boy. She was the first suffrage martyr in Central Asia. The woman suffrage movement did not begin with Mrs Pankhurst in the West, but with Ṭáhirih, also often called Qurratu'l-'Ayn of Írán. She was born in Qazvín, Persia, in 1817.

This was how Martha Root's talk began and it was clear as a bell, wasn't it? You will hear more of it tomorrow.

DAY 6

A Reading to Remember

O Companion of My Throne! Hear no evil, and see no evil, abase not thyself, neither sigh nor weep. Speak no evil, that thou mayest not hear it spoken unto thee …

Activity

Does your speech have a title yet? Sometimes you begin with a title that is exactly what you want to say and sometimes what the title should be becomes obvious only when you finish the speech.

Does every point you wrote have a sentence by it? Do some points need more than one sentence? How long do you want to make your speech?

Does three minutes sound okay? Were you trying for something longer? Nice and simple does it.

Now more from Miss Root's talk about Ṭáhirih:

> Náṣiri'd-Dín Sháh, the ruler, sent her (Ṭáhirih) a letter asking her to give up her very advanced ideas and telling her if she did, he would make her his bride, the greatest lady in the land. On the back of his letter she wrote her reply in verse declining his magnificently royal offer. Her words were:
> Kingdom, wealth and ruling be for thee,
> Wandering, becoming a poor dervish and calamity be for me.
> If that station is good, let it be for thee.
> And if this station is bad, I long for it, let it be for me!

For Reflection

Do you feel moved when you hear this poem? It was written a long time ago, in the middle of the 19th century.

A Reading to Remember

> O Companion of My Throne! Hear no evil, and see no evil, abase not thyself, neither sigh nor weep. Speak no evil, that thou mayest not hear it spoken unto thee …

Activity

The last of Martha Root's speech went like this:

> O Ṭáhirih, you have not passed out, you have only passed on! Your spiritual, courageous life will forever inspire, ennoble and refine humanity; your songs of the spirit will be treasured in innumerable hearts. You are to this day our living, thrilling teacher!

This was a very inspirational finish to her talk. Martha Root gave the listeners a lot to go away thinking about.

Now that you have heard about these two teachers, Ṭáhirih and Martha Root, draw pictures of their lives. Draw one for Ṭáhirih and one for Martha Root.

For Consultation

When you give your speech, what voice will you use? Will you use a big happy voice? Will you put a lot of feeling into what you are presenting? Discuss this with your teacher.

DAY 8

A Reading to Remember

O Companion of My Throne! Hear no evil, and see no evil, abase not thyself, neither sigh nor weep. Speak no evil, that thou mayest not hear it spoken unto thee, and magnify not the faults of others that thine own faults may not appear great …

Activity

Do a trial reading of your speech. Your teacher will help you begin to make the sentences sound right.

What would you do if you couldn't speak the language of the country you were in? Play a short game of charades with your teacher or with others. Remember, you will be using your hands because you can't understand the others and they can't understand you.

- Tell them it is a beautiful day and they don't need their umbrellas.
- 'Please make your dog stop licking my face!'
- 'Where is our lunch?'

DAY 9

A Reading to Remember

> O Companion of My Throne! Hear no evil, and see no evil, abase not thyself, neither sigh nor weep. Speak no evil, that thou mayest not hear it spoken unto thee, and magnify not the faults of others that thine own faults may not appear great ...

How is your memorization of this Hidden Word coming along?

Activity

Read your speech again and continue to add or take away the parts you need to change.

For Consultation

How do you speak to the members of your family?

DAY 10

A Reading to Remember

> O Companion of My Throne! Hear no evil, and see no evil, abase not thyself, neither sigh nor weep. Speak no evil, that thou mayest not hear it spoken unto thee, and magnify not the faults of others that thine own faults may not appear great; and wish not the abasement of anyone, that thine own abasement be not exposed.

Activity

Practise your speech again. Begin to use feelings to make it interesting and strong.

Ask your teacher to fix a time when you can give your speech to the members of your Bahá'í community, perhaps at a fireside or at a deepening class.

For Consultation

Do you wish to talk about anything today? Maybe you have a question or something might be going wrong that you would like some help with (besides your speech).

A Reading to Remember

O Companion of My Throne! Hear no evil, and see no evil, abase not thyself, neither sigh nor weep. Speak no evil, that thou mayest not hear it spoken unto thee, and magnify not the faults of others that thine own faults may not appear great; and wish not the abasement of anyone, that thine own abasement be not exposed.

Activity

Put your speech on a table and stand beside it so that you can see it. Begin to memorize the speech. Try little by little in the same way that you learn your prayers.

Instead of a consultation today, get extra help from your teacher as he listens to your speech. It seems like hard work but you will get there! Any time you have free you could practise it again.

A Reading to Remember

O Companion of My Throne! Hear no evil, and see no evil, abase not thyself, neither sigh nor weep. Speak no evil, that thou mayest not hear it spoken unto thee, and magnify not the faults of others that thine own faults may not appear great; and wish not the abasement of anyone, that thine own abasement be not exposed. Live then the days of thy life, that are less than a fleeting moment …

Activity

Go to a mirror. Put your paper down where you can see it but only if you look. Now look in the mirror and give your speech. How do you look? Try to improve your posture and look straight into the 'audience'. Do this once again when you have time. Remember to smile.

Now give your speech to your teacher again. Try not to use your notes. But if you do, just take it easy and don't get nervous.

DAY 13

A Reading to Remember

O Companion of My Throne! Hear no evil, and see no evil, abase not thyself, neither sigh nor weep. Speak no evil, that thou mayest not hear it spoken unto thee, and magnify not the faults of others that thine own faults may not appear great; and wish not the abasement of anyone, that thine own abasement be not exposed. Live then the days of thy life, that are less than a fleeting moment …

Activity

In the Hidden Word it says to speak no evil. If you speak no evil you will try to see the best in everything and everyone. The Hidden Word also says our own faults become greater when we discuss the faults we see in others. Put a few thoughts in your diary about a time when you spoke unkindly about someone else or when he or she spoke unkindly to you. This often happens when we lose our temper. We should understand that this really hurts us more than anything. It never helps to say hurtful things at all. After all, God loves everyone!

Act out a situation where three children are playing ball. Two children start giving the third (you) a hard time, saying you are the worst ball player they have ever seen and how they won't play with you ever again. What you say to them should be frank and honest but not nasty or hurtful. See whether you can answer them in a way that you would be proud of behaving.

For Consultation

Discuss being 'frank'. Being frank does not mean saying the first thing that comes into your mind. It needs thinking about and it takes a lot of courage but it saves a lot of future problems. What does your teacher think about it?

DAY 14

A Reading to Remember

O Companion of My Throne! Hear no evil, and see no evil, abase not thyself, neither sigh nor weep. Speak no evil, that thou mayest not hear it spoken unto thee, and magnify not the faults of others that thine own faults may not appear great; and wish not the abasement of anyone, that thine own abasement be not exposed. Live then the days of thy life, that are less than a fleeting moment, with thy mind stainless, thy heart unsullied, thy thoughts pure, and thy nature sanctified …

Activity

You might be an expert at giving your speech by now. Practise it again and make sure you feel confident with it.

There may well be a time very soon when you give your speech to people and enjoy all the work you put into it. Write down the speech in your diary. Be sure to use any opportunity to give the speech, especially if it is on a Bahá'í subject and helps to teach the Faith.

Choose one of your favourite Bahá'í songs to sing today. There are some lovely prayers put to music such as 'O God! Educate these children'.

DAY 15

A Reading to Remember

O Companion of My Throne! Hear no evil, and see no evil, abase not thyself, neither sigh nor weep. Speak no evil, that thou mayest not hear it spoken unto thee, and magnify not the faults of others that thine own faults may not appear great; and wish not the abasement of anyone, that thine own abasement be not exposed. Live then the days of thy life, that are less than a fleeting moment, with thy mind stainless, thy heart unsullied, thy thoughts pure, and thy nature sanctified …

Activity

This would be a nice time to have a special snack. Popcorn is good or some creamy custard or how about a plate of pancakes? Speak up and ask your teacher if she will have a snack with you. Then maybe you could listen to some music you like together.

If your teacher is on a Local Spiritual Assembly or goes to Bahá'í meetings she will know how important it is to speak fairly and honestly with your friends.

It achieves the best results. Maybe your teacher can explain to you how problems are solved this way.

A Reading to Remember

O Companion of My Throne! Hear no evil, and see no evil, abase not thyself, neither sigh nor weep. Speak no evil, that thou mayest not hear it spoken unto thee, and magnify not the faults of others that thine own faults may not appear great; and wish not the abasement of anyone, that thine own abasement be not exposed. Live then the days of thy life, that are less than a fleeting moment, with thy mind stainless, thy heart unsullied, thy thoughts pure, and thy nature sanctified, so that, free and content, thou mayest put away this mortal frame …

Activity

Bahá'u'lláh says we should keep our thoughts pure. This means lots of things. Draw a picture of some of your 'pure thoughts'.

For Consultation

Consult on the meaning of pure thoughts and how they make you feel contented.

A Reading to Remember

O Companion of My Throne! Hear no evil, and see no evil, abase not thyself, neither sigh nor weep. Speak no evil, that thou mayest not hear it spoken unto thee, and magnify not the faults of others that thine own faults may not appear great; and wish not the abasement of anyone, that thine own abasement be not exposed. Live then the days of thy life, that are less than a fleeting moment, with thy mind stainless, thy heart unsullied, thy thoughts pure, and thy nature sanctified, so that, free and content, thou mayest put away this mortal frame …

Activity

Let's make a kite today. (Maybe you can make something fancier but a diamond-shaped kite is fun.) Colour a large sheet of lightweight paper. Then take two long sticks for the frame, putting them into a 'T' shape. Tie them together with string. Then bind the paper around them in a diamond shape with some strong tape. Make a small hole in the bottom of the kite (the point of the V) and insert thin strips of cloth through to become the tail. Tie extra pieces of material to the tail so that there can be some balance. Where the wood is joined together you can get your teacher to help you attach the string which you hold when you fly the kite. This is a very basic kite and shouldn't be too hard to fly on a day with some wind. You can prepare for it just in case it's windy soon.

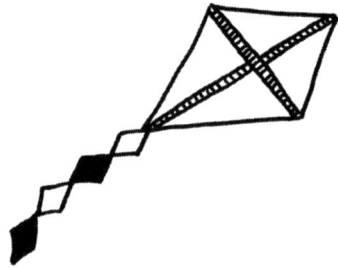

While flying your kite you can think about having freedom. Bahá'u'lláh says if we speak kindly of others and care about each other we will have pure minds, hearts and thoughts and that this helps us in this world and in the next.

DAY 18

A Reading to Remember

O Companion of My Throne! Hear no evil, and see no evil, abase not thyself, neither sigh nor weep. Speak no evil, that thou mayest not hear it spoken unto thee, and magnify not the faults of others that thine own faults may not appear great; and wish not the abasement of anyone, that thine own abasement be not exposed. Live then the days of thy life, that are less than a fleeting moment, with thy mind stainless, thy heart unsullied, thy thoughts pure, and thy nature sanctified, so that, free and content, thou mayest put away this mortal frame, and repair unto the mystic paradise …

Activity

Perhaps your parents won't mind if you hang your kite on your wall so that you remember how important your thoughts and your speech are to you.

Are you going to give your speech at the Feast? If so, you might like to say it once more just for your teacher. Hasn't she been a help to you!

DAY 19

A Reading to Remember

O Companion of My Throne! Hear no evil, and see no evil, abase not thyself, neither sigh nor weep. Speak no evil, that thou mayest not hear it spoken unto thee, and magnify not the faults of others that thine own faults may not appear great; and wish not the abasement of anyone, that thine own abasement be not exposed. Live then the days of thy life, that are less than a fleeting moment, with thy mind stainless, thy heart unsullied, thy thoughts pure, and thy nature sanctified, so that, free and content, thou mayest put away this mortal frame, and repair unto the mystic paradise and abide in the eternal kingdom for evermore.

Bahá'u'lláh

Activity

The Bahá'í fund is always there. Any time you feel you would like to make a little sacrifice, you can place your pocket money in your fund box and help so much happen in our world! It is wonderful to think that when all the Bahá'ís give to the fund it makes the Faith free (like your kite) to do so many things for humankind. You can take your box to the Feast and give it to the treasurer.

For Reflection

You have completed the month of Qawl. You have learned to give a speech, you have begun to understand keeping yourself free of bad speech and thought and, most of all, you have been serving Bahá'u'lláh. Onward to the month of Masá'il!

15
Month of Masá'il (Questions)

DAY 1

A Reading to Remember

Here is something special to learn and remember from *The Hidden Words*:

> O Son of Being! With the hands of power I made thee and with the fingers of strength I created thee; and within thee have I placed the essence of My light. Be thou content with it and seek naught else, for My work is perfect and My command is binding. Question it not, nor have a doubt thereof.
>
> *Bahá'u'lláh*

Activity

Using the reading above, try to work out a simple crossword puzzle. Use words from the reading and find a place where you can make a connection between the words, forming a pattern. This will take some thought! If this is too hard for you, perhaps you and your teacher can choose words from the reading that you can discuss.

For Consultation

People have lots of questions. Many of the most serious questions humankind has ever had to face will arise in the coming years. This month let's discuss some of these questions. You and your teacher should become familiar with them. Keep notes of your consultation.

A Reading to Remember

Learn to say this portion by heart.

O Son of Being!

Activity

Jobs and careers and occupations are important to people. One of the ways the world is going to have to change is that jobs will have to become more suited to people! Bahá'u'lláh has told us we must have an occupation or craft. At the present time, many people do not know which way to turn for a job. Many have no education and little choice of jobs. Many jobs are also wiped out when new technology is used. Some people work in very dangerous jobs, which they cannot do their whole life. Make a list of some jobs that you think may not be the same in the future, for example teaching. One idea for the future is that a teacher may live with his student for a time until he is happy with the student's progress. Then a new teacher would come with new lessons.

Use your imagination to think of new possibilities and situations. The example above is possible even though it sounds very different from what happens today. Work on these ideas for a few days.

For Consultation

If you get a few ideas about how jobs are changing, consult on them with your teacher. Make a chart of these ideas. When you've spent enough time on it, you can write a story about the society you have created!

A Reading to Remember

O Son of Being! With the hands of power I made thee …

Activity

Again, think of the needs of the world and design a job or two.

For Consultation

Discuss these with your teacher.

DAY 4

A Reading to Remember

O Son of Being! With the hands of power I made thee and with the fingers of strength I created thee …

Activity

Think about how jobs are changing. Who will carry away the rubbish? Who will look after the health of you and your family? What about your pets? What will happen to them? Farming will change. How would you change it? What will food be like? Will transport change? Keep imagining …

For Consultation

Discuss your ideas.

DAY 5

A Reading to Remember

O Son of Being! With the hands of power I made thee and with the fingers of strength I created thee …

Activity

Think about the future. Will you read newspapers? How will you read? Will you use a computer? Clothes may change. Think about clothes. Is exercise still a fun part of your life? Describe a job called 'exercise assistant'.

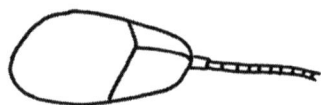

For Consultation

Discuss these ideas.

A Reading to Remember

O Son of Being! With the hands of power I made thee and with the fingers of strength I created thee …

Activity

Think about the future of our jobs. Will there be a spiritual element in them? In designing new jobs, make an effort to ensure that each job is wonderful spiritually! In the future, we hope that each person will be able to balance his spiritual needs and his material needs.

Here is a scenario to act out that might be a brand new idea. Jebbie goes to 'group doctor'. Group doctor sees Jebbie has a sad face. One doctor says he will check Jebbie for physical problems. Doctor Lulu says she will talk with Jebbie and see why he is not so happy. A third group doctor says he will work with Jebbie out in the fresh air to design a garden at the Elderly Park and see if this work does Jebbie some good. Now you decide the ending. Have Jebbie return a few days later and talk to the group doctor. How is Jebbie? Does he need anything else?

A Reading to Remember

O Son of Being! With the hands of power I made thee and with the fingers of strength I created thee; and within thee have I placed the essence of My light.

Activity

I hope the past few days of activity has been an inspiring and fun experience. Now begin to draft a story using all the jobs you created. List them. Make them 'real' with character names, give your story a plot and theme. Tomorrow you can write out a short story using these.

For Consultation

Is there an answer to every question?

A Reading to Remember

O Son of Being! With the hands of power I made thee and with the fingers of strength I created thee; and within thee have I placed the essence of My light.

Activity

Write your short story using yesterday's draft.

For Consultation

Read your story to your teacher and discuss it together.

DAY 9

A Reading to Remember

O Son of Being! With the hands of power I made thee and with the fingers of strength I created thee; and within thee have I placed the essence of My light. Be thou content with it and seek naught else …

Activity

Illustrate your story. Show the 'characters' and the work they do. Show and explain these drawings to your teacher.

DAY 10

A Reading to Remember

O Son of Being! With the hands of power I made thee and with the fingers of strength I created thee; and within thee have I placed the essence of My light. Be thou content with it and seek naught else …

Activity

What occupation do you intend to do? Write about this in your diary today. Has it changed since the last time you thought about this? Ask your teacher what you will need to prepare for your occupation. See if he thinks you have made a wise choice. Will this job still be necessary in the year 2020?

A Reading to Remember

O Son of Being! With the hands of power I made thee and with the fingers of strength I created thee; and within thee have I placed the essence of My light. Be thou content with it and seek naught else, for My work is perfect and My command is binding.

Activity

When some Bahá'ís visited 'Abdu'l-Bahá in the Holy Land, they asked Him many questions. These questions and His answers were put together in a book called Some Answered Questions. Many Bahá'ís study this book to learn the answers to questions about religion, life and the basic condition of our world.

Here is a lesson from this book, on the subject of true wealth:

> Then it is clear that the honour and exaltation of man must be something more than material riches. Material comforts are only a branch, but the root of the exaltation of man is the good attributes and virtues which are the adornments of his reality.
>
> 'Abdu'l-Bahá

'Abdu'l-Bahá goes on to explain that true wealth is doing the will of God, helping others and living a life of these kinds of comforts. Material comforts are not our goal.

For Consultation

When we go out to work, should part of our reward be a good feeling for the work we have done? Do people always feel like this now?

DAY 12

A Reading to Remember

O Son of Being! With the hands of power I made thee and with the fingers of strength I created thee; and within thee have I placed the essence of My light. Be thou content with it and seek naught else, for My work is perfect and My command is binding.

Activity

These words of 'Abdu'l-Bahá are so full of wisdom that we must read more! In this passage 'Abdu'l-Bahá talks about the difference between man and animal. Let your teacher read this paragraph to you. You will really have to listen but I am sure you will never forget this teaching of 'Abdu'l-Bahá:

> Praise be to God! man is always turned toward the heights, and his aspiration is lofty; he always desires to reach a greater world than the world in which he is, and to mount to a higher sphere than that in which he is. The love of exaltation is one of the characteristics of man. I am astonished that certain philosophers of America and Europe are content to gradually approach the animal world and so to go backward; for the tendency of existence must be toward exaltation. Nevertheless, if you said to one of them, 'You are an animal,' he would be extremely hurt and angry.
>
> *'Abdu'l-Bahá*

For Consultation

Before consulting on the above reading, make sure you are aware of the meaning of certain words: exaltation, sphere, aspiration, astonished, philosophers, tendency and characteristics. These are all rather advanced words for children to know and to use. Congratulations to you if you can!

DAY 13

A Reading to Remember

O Son of Being! With the hands of power I made thee and with the fingers of strength I created thee; and within thee have I placed the essence of My light. Be thou content with it and seek naught else, for My work is perfect and My command is binding. Question it not, nor have a doubt thereof.

Bahá'u'lláh

Activity

Another passage from Some Answered Questions for you to enjoy:

This world is also in the condition of a fruit tree, and man is like the fruit; without fruit the tree would be useless.

'Abdu'l-Bahá

Use your play dough to make a tree with little children as the fruit!

For Consultation

What do we have to do to make the 'fruit' of humankind the best it can be?

DAY 14

A Reading to Remember
Recite the whole Hidden Word you have been learning.

Activity
'Abdu'l-Bahá was asked, 'Should a criminal be punished, or forgiven and his crime overlooked?' You can read His answer in Some Answered Questions but, briefly, He said that communities must punish people who do the crimes so that others don't do the same thing. He also said that humankind needs to be educated so that people will never wish to commit a crime. But He said we should not punish in anger (vengeance). A person has no right to take vengeance. And, finally, 'Abdu'l-Bahá said how worthy it is for humans to forgive. He said forgiveness is one of the attributes of God.

For Consultation
What sort of education would teach us not to commit crime? How would you feel if you committed a crime?

DAY 15

A Reading to Remember
Recite the whole Hidden Word you have been learning.

Activity
For your activity write a few questions that you would like to ask at the Nineteen Day Feast or when adults can give you a bit of attention. Questions make everyone think and reflect. Your questions could be a real benefit to your community. Write three that your teacher agrees are especially interesting.

For Consultation

Laura Clifford Barney, the compiler of Some Answered Questions, referred to 'Abdu'l-Bahá as a 'teacher adapting Himself to His pupil, and not the orator or poet'. Perhaps your teacher could ponder this a while. With any student a teacher must be adaptable. Your teacher might reflect on how he feels when he teaches his students. Each student may grow up to bring radiance to society based on the instruction the teacher gives. Think of the example of 'Abdu'l-Bahá and the endless love He showed. Teacher, what would you like to say to your student today?

A Reading to Remember

Please say again the Hidden Word you have learned.

Activity

Find 19 beads, buttons or seeds and thread them onto a long chain, ribbon or string. Tie the ends together and you have a set of prayer beads! You can say 19 'Remover of Difficulties' or any other prayer without counting. You can also use them to say 'Alláh-u-Abhá' 95 times each day. Just count around your prayer beads five times. You could make some prayer beads for your friend's birthday or perhaps for Ayyám-i-Há or Naw-Rúz.

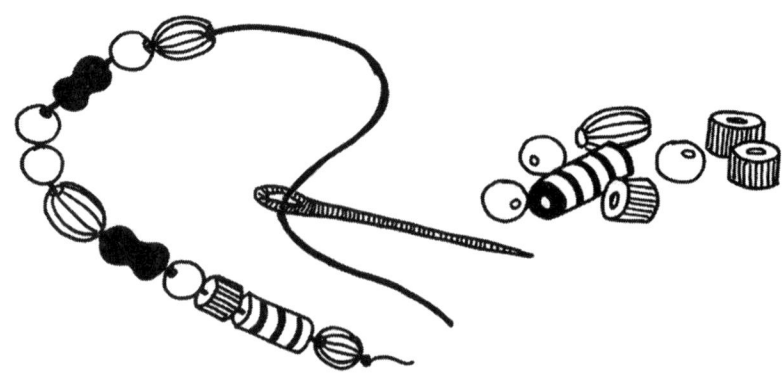

For Consultation

Here is a reading from 'Abdu'l-Bahá:

> The honour of man is through the attainment of the knowledge of God; his happiness is from the love of God; his joy is in the glad tidings of God; his greatness is dependent upon his servitude to God.
>
> *'Abdu'l-Bahá*

Does this sum up for you the purpose of spending these few minutes a day together?

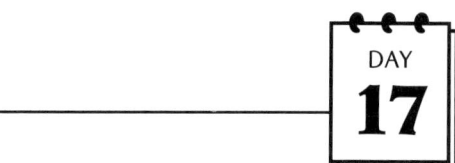

A Reading to Remember

Please say again the Hidden Word that you have learned.

Activity

Is there anyone in your neighbourhood you could go and visit? Why don't you and your teacher visit that person now. Spread a little happiness.

How was your visit? It's nice to make other people happy.

A Reading to Remember

Please say your Hidden Word again.

Activity

Try to answer these questions:

1. How many months are there in the Bahá'í calendar?
2. What year did the Báb declare Himself?
3. We have studied some beautiful readings from a book called The Hidden _____ .
4. There are guides that we live by. Some are called laws and some are called principles. One of the principles is the _____ of men and women.
5. A principle of the Bahá'í Faith is universal compulsory _____ .
6. Where was Bahá'u'lláh was born and in what year?
7. Bahá'í s must _____ to God every day.
8. If we say something unkind about someone when he is not there it is called _____ .
9. Bahá'u'lláh came to bring the _____ of humankind.

The answers are at the end of the month.

For Consultation

Discuss any of the answers you did not know.

A Reading to Remember

Please say your Hidden Word for the last time this month.

Activity

Read this passage from a letter of the International Teaching Centre dated 5 December 1988:

> One of the serious questions which the Institutions of the Cause of God must take up afresh is how to assist the children of the world. The children of the world at this time have a destiny before God.

For Consultation

Discuss with your teacher what can be done to help the children of the world? What does it mean that children have a destiny before God? Think of what you have just discussed. End this Bahá'í month with a prayer of your choice.

Answers

1. 19 2. 1844 3. Words 4. equality 5. education 6. Persia (or Iran) in 1817 7. pray 8. backbiting 9. unity

16

Month of S͟haraf
(Honour)

A Reading to Remember

Say, O My people! Show honour to your parents and pay homage to them. This will cause blessings to descend upon you from the clouds of the bounty of your Lord, the Exalted, the Great.

Bahá'u'lláh

Activity

Please get your dictionary and look up the word 'honour'. Mine says 'high respect, nobleness of mind, exalted position'. Read through all of the definitions with your teacher.

For Consultation

Baha'u'llah says we are to honour our parents. One way to understand this is that they have an exalted station in our eyes. Another way to understand this is that we should show them true respect. Discuss these ideas. Does this mean you should not argue with your parents? Does it mean your parents are your servants? Does it mean your parents are special?

A Reading to Remember

Learn these words of Bahá'u'lláh by heart. You can do this by reciting them and remembering them during each day.

> Say, O My people! Show honour to your parents …

Activity

In your diary write a short report about how you feel about honouring your own parents. Would you like to treat them more honourably? Do you feel happy about your behaviour now?

For Consultation

One way of thinking about honouring our parents is to obey them. Could this also be obedience to God? What do you think about this?

A Reading to Remember

> Say, O My people! Show honour to your parents and pay homage to them. This will cause blessings to descend upon you …

Activity

Let's try to understand our parents. Get some glue and enough paper to cut several thin but strong strips. Make the strips the same length and put them in a little pile. Is your glue ready? Have you ever made a paper chain? You make a loop with one piece of paper. You glue it into that shape. Then you hold the loop and put a new piece of paper through the loop and glue it into another loop. The two are connected, aren't they? Interesting!

Make another loop and then another. Keep going for a while and soon you will have a long chain of loops. This is like the generations of humankind in a way. One long chain of parents, children, parents, children, etc. You couldn't be a child unless you had a parent. It is a cycle.

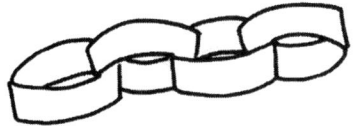

For Consultation

Ask your teacher to make this idea clear to you if you think your loops only look like loops and your chain is not at all helpful in understanding your parents.

DAY 4

A Reading to Remember

Say, O My people! Show honour to your parents and pay homage to them. This will cause blessings to descend upon you from the clouds of the bounty …

Activity

Look at your paper chain. Think of the first loop as yourself and the second one as your parents, the third one as your grandparents, the fourth one as your great grandparents and so on. Now suppose your great grandparents had no children. Would you be here? Were they important to you? Maybe you never knew them but they affected your life completely.

For Consultation

Consult on this and think about all these people in your family you never knew.

A Reading to Remember

Say, O My people! Show honour to your parents and pay homage to them. This will cause blessings to descend upon you from the clouds of the bounty of your Lord, the Exalted, the Great.

Bahá'u'lláh

Activity

Take another look at your paper chain. Your family chain started a long way back in the past and is part of the whole history of humankind! If you knew the stories of all the people who were your ancestors, it would be like a book of the history of the planet.

Write a pretend story about some people in your family who lived, say, in the time of Jesus Christ. If you need some help, you can use the Bible to get an idea of how people lived then. Take time and enjoy writing a story that you like.

For Consultation

If you saw this pretend family member come from the past into your kitchen right now, don't you think you would be very interested and respectful to him or her? Surely you would want to listen and ask questions and really take notice of what he or she was saying! So what would your answer be to this? When your mother and father talk to you do you show them the respect of listening to them with eagerness?

DAY 6

A Reading to Remember

Say the entire reading by heart, if you can.

Activity

Write more about your family history. Either continue the story or just make some character sketches of other possible members of your past family (ancestors). If you need help with writing, ask your teacher – politely!

For Consultation

What is honourable about our past? Why are our ancestors and parents treated with honour? Can you think why we should also treat our teachers with honour? It seems we should treat with honour those people who nurture us and care for us. Without them, as we have found, we would not be!

DAY 7

A Reading to Remember

Can you say your reading by heart?

Activity

Today listen to this story by Gloria Faizi and perhaps the kind of honour shown by 'Abdu'l-Bahá to Louis Gregory will be the kind of honour you will show to your friends:

> Once when 'Abdu'l-Bahá was in Washington DC He invited a black American friend, Mr Gregory, to come to the house of a high government official who was giving a luncheon party in honour of 'Abdu'l-Bahá. Mr Gregory was surprised because he knew he had

not been invited to the lunch and he also knew that it was not the custom for white Americans to eat with a black man. However, he felt he must go if the Master wished to see him. 'Abdu'l-Bahá met him with His usual kindness. For an hour they talked of many things. Suddenly the servant appeared at the door and announced, 'Lunch is served.' 'Abdu'l-Bahá got up quickly and went to the dining room but Mr Gregory stayed behind, not knowing what he should do. Should he leave or should he wait?

'Abdu'l-Bahá went to the table, stopped suddenly and in a rather loud voice He said, in English, 'Where is my friend, Mr Gregory? My friend Mr Gregory must lunch with me.'

There was only one thing to do. The servant went in search of Mr Gregory. In the meantime, 'Abdu'l-Bahá began pushing aside the many knives and forks and glasses to make a place beside Himself for Mr Gregory.

So Mr Gregory sat in the place of honour beside 'Abdu'l-Bahá at the table. And 'Abdu'l-Bahá entertained the party in such a delightful way that soon all the guests forgot, at least for a while, anything so stupid as disliking another human being merely because of the colour of his skin.

For Consultation

What do you think of this story?

DAY 8

Reading

Thus should it be among the children of men! The diversity in the human family should be the cause of love and harmony, as it is in music where many different notes blend together in the making of a perfect chord. If you meet those of different race and colour from yourself, do not mistrust them and withdraw yourself into your shell of conventionality, but rather be glad and show them kindness. Think of them as different coloured roses growing in the beautiful garden of humanity, and rejoice to be among them.

'Abdu'l-Bahá

Activity

Imagine lots and lots of paper chains in a big room or hanging from a huge old tree. Only one of them would be 'your family' but all of the chains would be part of the total beauty of the world of paper chains. Some might be very different and others not too different from yours but all are just as necessary to the paper chain world. We would miss the different ones if they weren't there. Draw different faces on each link of your paper chain.

For Consultation

So we should honour not only our wonderful parents, our terrific teachers and the different people of the world but we see by now that Bahá'u'lláh means for us to honour everyone. We should look for the good things about each person and not separate ourselves from them just because they have a different point of view or look and act differently from us. That is a lot to think about. What would you like to discuss with your teacher about this subject?

A Prayer to Remember

O God, teach us Thy Oneness and give us a realization of Thy Unity, that we may see no one save Thee. Thou art the Merciful and the Giver of bounty!

Bahá'u'lláh

Activity

Today make a little flower garden with your play dough. Plant lots of different flowers in a flower box and let it dry out. You can paint the flowers different colours later and remind yourself that although we all look different, each one should honour the other.

For Reflection

If we took all the paper chains we imagined and hooked them all together they would be one huge paper chain, right? There would be one paper chain, which would make them all united. Bahá'u'lláh wants us to see unity and God in everything we do. We come from the same source (which is God) and He wishes us to be united. We cannot be united unless we honour each other.

A Prayer to Remember

O God, teach us Thy Oneness and give us a realization of Thy Unity, that we may see no one save Thee.

Activity

Have you ever made a garden salad? Ask your parents if you can make one. Choose a few vegetables and other things and construct a delicious salad. You could use some cooked pasta, beans, rice or meat, some fresh garden greens such as lettuce, herbs, cucumbers or other vegetables and add to this some tomatoes, pepper, onion, garlic, vinegar, oil, spice and on and on, depending on what your family likes.

For Consultation

When you look at the salad and see all the different ingredients, you see how each one complements the other. Life can be like that. Discuss the variety of life.

DAY 11

A Prayer to Remember

O God, teach us Thy Oneness and give us a realization of Thy Unity, that we may see no one save Thee. Thou art the Merciful and the Giver of bounty!

Bahá'u'lláh

Activity

Once we have learned to honour God and humankind, we can be sure that peace will follow. World peace is a reality that Bahá'ís believe in. Many people currently believe that this is impossible. For your activity, interview your teacher, as if you were on the radio. Let her tell you how to have world peace. To get you started, here are three questions for you to ask her 'on the air':

1. What is peace?
2. Who makes peace first?
3. What is so good about a peaceful person?

Pretend that in the middle of your radio interview yesterday someone rang the producer and said he didn't believe what you were saying about peace because he liked to fight and didn't want to be peaceful. You are back on the air and speaking to this person. What do you want to say to him?

For Consultation

How do you treat a person who doesn't like you at all and who makes trouble for you? How can we be understanding when people don't agree with what we believe as Bahá'ís? Does it hurt your feelings that they do not honour what you believe? This could be something to remember your whole life.

A Reading

In the garden of thy heart plant naught but the rose of love …

Bahá'u'lláh

Following this reading solves many of the difficulties of life. First of all, if a child could learn this love, he would face difficulties like a mighty warrior! With the love of God, he could conquer anything!

Activity

Make yourself a suit of armour. Make it with anything you happen to have on hand. You can drape a sheet around yourself. Take a walk. What is this armour? Of course, the love of God! How does it feel to have this special love-suit on? Can people see it?

For Consultation

What do people see when you show them love?

A Prayer to Remember

Can you say by heart the prayer you learned this month?

Activity

Write a letter to your pen pal again. Maybe you could tell your friend about what you have learned about honouring your parents. You could mention that you made a flower garden. Then perhaps you can include the reading you read today. This letter will be full of the kind of love that makes a real friendship.

For Consultation

If it's possible to walk to the post box with your teacher, do so. This will give you the chance to talk more about the attribute of honour. Why did Bahá'u'lláh give us a month of honour?

A Prayer to Remember

Recite the prayer you learned this month.

Activity

Bahá'ís know that our deeds are more important than our words. Offer to do something for your parents today and tell them it is your way of showing that you appreciate them and honour them. You could even write them a poem or note. You could wash dishes. Your teacher can guide you.

For Consultation

Do you realize that there is a world full of children who believe in Bahá'í principles? They're not just for a few people. You may be one of the few people in your school who know about the Bahá'í Faith but many people want peace and unity in the world. It is good to remember that things are getting better all the time. All the children who learn principles to live by will one day be adults and may well be the rulers of cities and even countries. What does your teacher say about this?

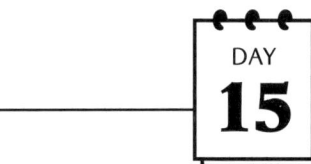

A Prayer to Remember

Say the prayer you learned this month.

Activity

Is there an organization you can be a part of that helps your community live better? So many people need some kind of help. Discuss with your teacher what you can do to help. For your activity, make some decisions about this.

For Reflection

How did you choose something you can do? When will you begin to do your 'job'? How do you feel?

A Prayer to Remember

Say your prayer for this month.

Activity

In your diary, record what you intend to do. Have you contacted the group or person who can get you started on your community work? Write in your diary how it feels to be helping. You may find you are doing a job but feel like it is just for fun!

For Consultation

What is the best reason for helping other people?

A Prayer to Remember
Say your prayer for this month.

Activity
Play a 'Good Feelings' game with your teacher. Make up things you can do that give you good feelings. Compare this to the game of Monopoly!

For Consultation
What would we do if we had no money to get all the things we need? People used to trade things. What would you give me if I gave you an apple? What would you give me if I gave you a baseball bat? How about a baseball and we could have a game?

A Prayer to Remember
Say your prayer for this month.

Activity
Here is another story by Gloria Faizi about what we really need!

> Often when the family of 'Abdu'l-Bahá was about to sit down to dinner at night in 'Akká, He would receive a report that some unfortunate person was starving. Without question, the family

would quickly pack their own meal in a basket and send it away to the suffering family. At such times, 'Abdu'l-Bahá would smile and say, 'It does not matter for us. We had dinner last night and we shall have dinner again tomorrow.'

For Consultation

When we think about doing things to help our community, we find many people less fortunate than ourselves. We get the chance to sacrifice things that we have for them. We actually give these things to God. What does this mean?

DAY 19

A Prayer to Remember

Say your prayer for this month for the last time.

Activity

You have finished the month of Honour. In the Bahá'í calendar it is called Sharaf. Draw a picture of yourself doing the job you chose to do, or if you are little, draw yourself and a job you can do at home. Now that you are helping someone else, you are starting an honourable pattern for your life!

For Reflection

Please don't forget that a unified and peaceful world begins with you and your attitude to everyone you meet. This should begin with your home and your favourite people – your Mum, your Dad, your family.

17

Month of Sulṭán
(Sovereignty)

DAY 1

A Prayer to Remember

Praised be Thou, O Lord my God! Graciously grant that this infant be fed from the breast of Thy tender mercy and loving providence and be nourished with the fruit of Thy celestial trees. Suffer him not to be committed to the care of anyone save Thee, inasmuch as Thou, Thyself, through the potency of Thy sovereign will and power, didst create and call him into being. There is none other God but Thee, the Almighty, the All-Knowing.

Bahá'u'lláh

Activity

Ask your teacher to read you a story of Badí'. One can be found in the introduction to *Epistle to the Son of the Wolf* or you might have one written especially for children.

For Consultation

Was Badí' brave? The story in *Epistle to the Son of the Wolf* says that Badí' was 'recreated'. What does this mean?

Day 2

A Prayer to Remember

Learn this section of the prayer by heart. By doing this you will be able to recite it all by the end of the month of Sovereignty.

> Praised be Thou, O Lord my God!

Activity

Today sing 'Shine Your Light on Me', if you know it. Here are the words:

> Shine your light on me, Bahá'u'lláh,
> I am over here, Bahá'u'lláh
> Shine your light on me, Bahá'u'lláh
> Glori-ay! Glori-ay!
>
> Let me be a lamp, Bahá'u'lláh
> (etc.)
>
> We can teach the world, Bahá'u'lláh
> (etc.)

For Consultation

Do you think Bahá'u'lláh can hear you when you sing this song (or any song) to Him with all your heart? Why or why not?

A Prayer to Remember

Learn this section of the prayer by heart.

> Praised be Thou, O Lord my God! Graciously grant that this infant be fed …

Activity

Play act something you could do to help your king, president or prime minister. Remember the bravery of Badí'? Think of a skit in which you do something wonderful for your king.

For Consultation

Discuss this Hidden Word:

> O My Servant! Abandon not for that which perisheth an everlasting dominion, and cast not away celestial sovereignty for a worldly desire. This is the river of everlasting life that hath flowed from the well-spring of the pen of the merciful; well is it with them that drink!
>
> *Bahá'u'lláh*

Ask your teacher or parent to explain this Hidden Word in his words. When you feel you understand at least one of the meanings, discuss it.

A Prayer to Remember

Praised be Thou, O Lord my God! Graciously grant that this infant be fed from the breast of Thy tender mercy …

Activity

Thinking of the Hidden Word you heard yesterday, draw a picture of a river of everlasting life. At the bottom of the picture write what it is like to drink from it. How does it taste? Decorate the picture.

For Consultation

What is the difference between a 'celestial sovereignty' and a worldly one? Your teacher or parent can explain the words to you first.

DAY 5

A Prayer to Remember

Praised be Thou, O Lord my God! Graciously grant that this infant be fed from the breast of Thy tender mercy and loving providence …

Activity

Make a cardboard crown. When you decorate it, think of the different attributes your king will need and label the crown with them. Perhaps you could wear this crown to the next Nineteen Day Feast and tell the community about it!

For Consultation

What is the definition of 'sovereignty'? My dictionary says 'possessing power, royal, lofty'. A sovereign has supreme power. This is one of the attributes of God.

DAY 6

A Prayer to Remember

Praised be Thou, O Lord my God! Graciously grant that this infant be fed from the breast of Thy tender mercy and loving providence and be nourished with the fruit of Thy celestial trees.

Activity

Build a castle. Make it out of play dough or cardboard or sticks and paper. Or perhaps you could draw one.

For Consultation

Another dictionary meaning of sovereignty is 'complete independence'. If God is completely independent of us, it follows that whatever we do is not going to change Him or His sovereignty. He can change us and our world but we can only serve Him, not affect Him. Does this sound right to you? Consult about this.

A Prayer to Remember

Praised be Thou, O Lord my God! Graciously grant that this infant be fed from the breast of Thy tender mercy and loving providence and be nourished with the fruit of Thy celestial trees.

Activity

Yesterday you made a castle. It probably is very secure and solid! Now make some objects that might be kept there – some valuable things for a king.

For Consultation

Just as a king may desire to have some objects in his castle, so Bahá'u'lláh tells us God desires things from us. If we are loyal servants of God, what do we give Him? What do we do for Him to please Him?

A Prayer to Remember

Praised be Thou, O Lord my God! Graciously grant that this infant be fed from the breast of Thy tender mercy and loving providence and be nourished with the fruit of Thy celestial trees. Suffer him not to be committed to the care of anyone save Thee …

Activity

The Universal House of Justice meets in a wonderful building at the Bahá'í World Centre. It looks more beautiful than a castle but it holds what Bahá'u'lláh has brought to this world in the name of God. To the Bahá'ís of the world it holds the greatest hope for humanity. A king could never possess this sort of a kingdom. Make a collage, using magazine cutouts or drawings of world rulers – not just kings and queens but prime ministers, presidents, etc. If you have a photograph of the Shrine of the Báb or the Shrine of Bahá'u'lláh, you could circle the Shrine with the collage of photos.

For Consultation

One day all of the rulers of the world will come to the Bahá'í World Centre and the world will change. What do you think will happen? Imagine this.

A Prayer to Remember

Praised be Thou, O Lord my God! Graciously grant that this infant be fed from the breast of Thy tender mercy and loving providence and be nourished with the fruit of Thy celestial trees. Suffer him not to be committed to the care of anyone save Thee …

Activity

Bahá'u'lláh has written:

> Call out to Zion, O Carmel, and announce the joyful tidings: He that was hidden from mortal eyes is come! His all-conquering sovereignty is manifest; His all-encompassing splendour is revealed. Beware lest thou hesitate or halt. Hasten forth and circumambulate the City of God that hath descended from heaven, the celestial Kaaba round which have circled in adoration the favoured of God, the pure in heart, and the company of the most exalted angels. Oh, how I long to announce unto every spot on the surface of the earth, and to carry to each one of its cities, the glad-tidings of this Revelation – a

Revelation to which the heart of Sinai hath been attracted, and in whose name the Burning Bush is calling: 'Unto God, the Lord of Lords, belong the kingdoms of earth and heaven'. Verily this is the Day in which both land and sea rejoice at this announcement, the Day for which have been laid up those things which God, through a bounty beyond the ken of mortal mind or heart, hath destined for revelation. Ere long will God sail His Ark upon thee, and will manifest the people of Bahá who have been mentioned in the Book of Names.

For Consultation

Today you have worked on memorizing your prayer and read the above passage from the Tablet of Carmel. If you become familiar with the language and think of this Tablet, you may learn a lot about sovereignty.

DAY 10

A Prayer to Remember

Praised be Thou, O Lord my God! Graciously grant that this infant be fed from the breast of Thy tender mercy and loving providence and be nourished with the fruit of Thy celestial trees. Suffer him not to be committed to the care of anyone save Thee, inasmuch as Thou, Thyself …

Activity

Let's study another passage from the Bahá'í teachings today.

I consider it my duty to warn every beginner in the Faith that the promised glories of the Sovereignty which the Bahá'í teachings foreshadow, can be revealed only in the fullness of time, that the implications of the Aqdas and the Will of 'Abdu'l-Bahá, as the twin repositories of the constituent elements of the Sovereignty, are too far-reaching for this generation to grasp and fully appreciate. I cannot refrain from appealing to them who stand identified with the Faith to disregard the prevailing notions and the fleeting fashions of the day, and to realize as never before that the exploded theories and the tottering institutions of present-day civilization must needs appear in sharp contrast with those God-given institutions which are destined to arise upon their ruin.

Shoghi Effendi

Your teacher can help you understand this by explaining some of the words and ideas in it.

For Consultation

One thing this passage says is that we are not able to understand the total picture of the sovereignty of the Bahá'í Revelation. When children learn about the world, they learn step by step. The whole world is learning about the Bahá'í Revelation in this way. Discuss this with your teacher.

DAY 11

A Prayer to Remember

Praised be Thou, O Lord my God! Graciously grant that this infant be fed from the breast of Thy tender mercy and loving providence and be nourished with the fruit of Thy celestial trees. Suffer him not to be committed to the care of anyone save Thee, inasmuch as Thou, Thyself, through the potency of Thy sovereign will and power …

Activity

If you have an encyclopedia, look up the United Nations in it. Or perhaps you have a book about it.

For Consultation

What do you know about the United Nations? Who belongs to it? Where is it located? What does it do?

DAY 12

A Prayer to Remember

Praised be Thou, O Lord my God! Graciously grant that this infant be fed from the breast of Thy tender mercy and loving providence and be nourished with the fruit of Thy celestial trees. Suffer him not to be committed to the care of anyone save Thee, inasmuch as Thou, Thyself, through the potency of Thy sovereign will and power …

Activity

If possible, make this a family time today. Your family is your own little 'kingdom' and your home is your 'castle'. One thing that is always fun for the family is 'Question Time'. Perhaps the parents can ask the children some questions about the Faith and give a star for a correct answer. Or the children could ask hard questions to the parents and give them stars. Or the whole family could have a consultation period during which everyone would share their ideas about a subject. If you can't do this, spend the time with your teacher the same way!

DAY 13

A Prayer to Remember

Praised be Thou, O Lord my God! Graciously grant that this infant be fed from the breast of Thy tender mercy and loving providence and be nourished with the fruit of Thy celestial trees. Suffer him not to be committed to the care of anyone save Thee, inasmuch as Thou, Thyself, through the potency of Thy sovereign will and power, didst create and call him into being.

Activity

The work of teaching children is very special. 'Abdu'l-Bahá had this to say about it:

> O thou teacher of the children of the kingdom! Thou hast arisen to perform a service which would justly entitle thee to vaunt thyself over all the teachers on earth. For the teachers of this world make use of human education to develop the powers, whether spiritual or material, of humankind, whilst thou art training these young plants in the gardens of God according to the education of Heaven, and art giving them the lessons of the Kingdom. The result of this kind of teaching will be that it will attract the blessings of God, and make manifest the perfections of man.
>
> Hold thou fast to this kind of teaching, for the fruits of it will be very great. The children must, from their infancy, be raised to be spiritual and godly Bahá'ís. If such be their training, they will remain safe from every test.
>
> *'Abdu'l-Bahá*

Think about this for a while.

For Consultation

Please discuss the passage between yourselves. Being a teacher is a gift from God but so is being a student! The education you give and receive will 'attract the blessings of God'. What do you think about this reading?

DAY 14

A Prayer to Remember

> Praised be Thou, O Lord my God! Graciously grant that this infant be fed from the breast of Thy tender mercy and loving providence and be nourished with the fruit of Thy celestial trees. Suffer him not to be committed to the care of anyone save Thee, inasmuch as Thou, Thyself, through the potency of Thy sovereign will and power, didst create and call him into being.

Activity

You know what it's like to learn and be taught something. But did you realize that you teach other children? Through your example and attitude, they learn from you. For example, if you have courage and stay away from the harmful things of life, they learn that it is possible for them to do this too. One of the features of the Bahá'í lifestyle is that it is safe. List some of the 'safe' things Bahá'ís do.

For Consultation

Consult on this list with your teacher and see if there are any more additions.

DAY 15

A Prayer to Remember

Praised be Thou, O Lord my God! Graciously grant that this infant be fed from the breast of Thy tender mercy and loving providence and be nourished with the fruit of Thy celestial trees. Suffer him not to be committed to the care of anyone save Thee, inasmuch as Thou, Thyself, through the potency of Thy sovereign will and power, didst create and call him into being. There is none other God but Thee …

Activity

All of us have been created the same by God yet some people do not seem to believe this. When you are at school and you see someone who needs help, what do you do? Write about an experience you have had.

For Consultation

What does your teacher think about how you handled the above situation?

DAY 16

A Prayer to Remember

Praised be Thou, O Lord my God! Graciously grant that this infant be fed from the breast of Thy tender mercy and loving providence and be nourished with the fruit of Thy celestial trees. Suffer him not to be committed to the care of anyone save Thee, inasmuch as Thou, Thyself, through the potency of Thy sovereign will and power, didst create and call him into being. There is none other God but Thee, the Almighty, the All-Knowing.

Bahá'u'lláh

Activity

School becomes a very large part of a child's life. Only a few years ago – and even now in some countries – school was a luxury very few children were able to have. You might like to think about what you would be doing if you had no school. You would probably be working and doing adult jobs! It's really lucky you can go to school and learn. If school is going to help you, what will it teach you?

For Consultation

What can you do to help your school? Is there something you would like to offer to do?

DAY 17

A Prayer to Remember

Can you say the prayer you have been learning by heart?

Activity

How about writing a letter to your pen pal? Do you enjoy expressing yourself and writing about what you have learned? When you exchange ideas with your friend you teach each other.

For Consultation

Your town or city is an important part of your life. You probably know people who work there and sell things to you or serve you.

What if people didn't bother to build anything? Where would you get the things you need?

Why do people live in one place together? Does it help them to work together? If you wanted to buy a toy and there was no toy store, you couldn't buy a toy, could you?

DAY 18

A Prayer to Remember

Recite the prayer you have been learning this month.

Activity

There are people who rule, or govern, your town or city or area. What if no one looked after your town? Where would the rubbish go? Who would keep order and maintain safety? What would happen to a visitor? Write about a town with no order.

For Consultation

We only expect what we have learned to expect. Things change all the time and they change because people need change. What one thing do you think would be a good change for your town?

DAY 19

A Prayer to Remember

Recite the prayer for this month. Congratulations on learning it!

Activity

This is the last day of the month of Sovereignty and we have looked at many different aspects of sovereignty. When you go to the Nineteen Day Feast you might remember to wear the crown you made this month and explain the values of sovereignty which you have learned. The friends will probably be very interested to hear what you have been working on. Collect your ideas and work out how to share them now so that they will be ready for the Feast.

For Consultation

Sovereignty is an attribute of God. No matter what happens in our life we can be sure that He is looking after us and our best interests. We can all look after the best interests of each other as well. Discuss this.

18

Month of Mulk
(Dominion)

DAY 1

A Reading to Remember

During the next week learn these words of Bahá'u'lláh by heart:

> Lo, the All-Possessing is come. Earth and heaven, glory and dominion are God's, the Lord of all men, and the Possessor of the Throne on high and of earth below!
>
> *Bahá'u'lláh*

Activity

Can you draw a picture of your idea of a 'throne on high'?

For Consultation

Is there anything that doesn't belong to God?

DAY 2

A Reading to Remember

Lo, the All-Possessing is come. Earth and heaven, glory and dominion are God's, the Lord of all men, and the Possessor of the Throne on high and of earth below!

Bahá'u'lláh

Activity

You have probably heard the phrase 'The earth is but one country'. Draw a map of this country. Where would you put the 'capital'? You can make this map using your imagination or you can trace or copy a map of the world.

For Consultation

Who rules the dominion of earth? Where is the home of this ruler?

DAY 3

A Reading to Remember

Lo, the All-Possessing is come.

Activity

Please get your dictionary. In my dictionary dominion means 'control or the exercise of control', 'rule', 'sovereignty', 'a territory or sphere of influence', 'realm' or 'domain'. What does your dictionary say? Do these definitions go along with what we have been learning in our lessons?

For Consultation

Read this prayer from the Bible. It is known as the Lord's Prayer:

Our Father which art in heaven, hallowed be thy name. Thy kingdom come. Thy will be done in earth, as it is in heaven.

Give us this day our daily bread. And forgive us our debts, as we forgive our debtors. And lead us not into temptation, but deliver us from evil: For thine is the kingdom, and the power, and the glory, for ever. Amen.

The Lord's Prayer, which came to us with Christianity, has been prayed for 2000 years. Now the 'kingdom of God' is coming about through the Bahá'í Revelation. With the blueprint given by Bahá'u'lláh, 'the kingdom of God' on earth 'as it is in heaven' will be a reality. Consult on the fact that the kingdom of heaven and earth are united.

A Reading to Remember

Lo, the All-Possessing is come. Earth and heaven, glory and dominion are God's …

Activity

Have you studied space? Draw a picture of our solar system or make models of planets from play dough. Does God's dominion go further than this solar system?

For Consultation

Where does a dominion end? A king might rule a certain part of the earth but someone else rules the country next to his. Where does God's dominion end or begin?

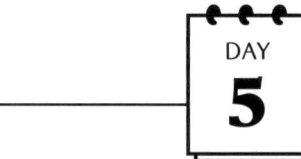

A Reading to Remember

Lo, the All-Possessing is come. Earth and heaven, glory and dominion are God's, the Lord of all men …

Activity

Have you ever gone fishing? If you can't go out to a waterway and fish (with an adult) then try filling up the bathtub and throwing in some waterproof toys. Get a big spoon or ladle and go fishing. You need to be skilled to catch fish but it is also necessary for fish to be in the water before you can catch them. When you fish in the river, you can't see the fish, unlike your bathtub, where the 'fish' are in clear view. Do you like fishing?

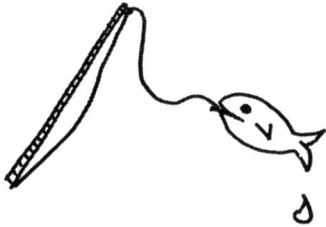

For Consultation

Why do people fish? Is it a challenge? Why do people need challenges?

DAY 6

A Reading to Remember

Lo, the All-Possessing is come. Earth and heaven, glory and dominion are God's, the Lord of all men, and the Possessor of the Throne on high and of earth below!

Bahá'u'lláh

Activity

Take some building blocks. Almost everyone likes to build and it is a challenge to build a tower as high as possible. If you have enough blocks, you could race against your teacher.

For Consultation

What sort of challenge do you enjoy? Do you like to compete against yourself or do you enjoy competing with your friend? What is more important – to win or to appreciate the game?

DAY 7

A Reading to Remember
Recite the whole passage you have learned this week. Were you successful in memorizing it?

Activity
Think of something you can do in your life to challenge yourself. Ask your teacher to help you think of something. You could ask a friend to do the same thing and compete against each other, each one trying to do his best!

For Consultation
When we see chances in life to do our best, we should take them. Our skill will constantly grow if we allow it to do so. Ask any fisherman!

DAY 8

A Reading to Remember
Recite once more the passage you learned this week.

Activity
Have you ever envied anyone for his great ability or because he won something? It is not good to envy others; rather, we should love each other and be happy for each other. In *The Hidden Words* Bahá'u'lláh says:

> O Son of Earth! Know, verily, the heart wherein the least remnant of envy yet lingers, shall never attain My everlasting dominion, nor inhale the sweet savours of holiness breathing from My kingdom of sanctity.
>
> *Bahá'u'lláh*

For Consultation

Ask your teacher or parent to explain this to you.

A Reading to Remember

Do you remember the importance of these words of Bahá'u'lláh? Learn the Hidden Word you read yesterday by memorizing a portion each day.

    O Son of Earth!

Activity

One of the saddest things in life to see is someone who has become greedy. Greed overcomes common sense and the challenge of having more of this or that thing becomes more important than any thought of moderation or healthy competition. Here are some of the things people become greedy about: food, money, love, friendship, toys, achievement at school, art. You might make a longer list.

For Consultation

Discuss with your teacher or parent the ways in which people can become greedy about these things. Remember, although it is a challenge to do your best, 'your best' is of no benefit if you have to be better than everyone else to enjoy yourself.

A Reading to Remember

O Son of Earth! Know, verily, the heart wherein the least remnant of envy yet lingers …

Activity

Have a little picnic today with your teacher. Go outside, relax and be happy enjoying the dominion of God!

For Consultation

Discuss the beauty of God's dominion.

A Reading to Remember

O Son of Earth! Know, verily, the heart wherein the least remnant of envy yet lingers …

Activity

God loves us very much, so much that He sent us into this world. Even when we are dead we still are part of His dominion. He doesn't leave us floating around somewhere; He welcomes us back to Him.

Listen to this prayer, which is written for the dead:

> O my God, Thy Trust hath been returned unto Thee. It behoveth Thy grace and Thy bounty that have compassed Thy dominions on earth and in heaven, to vouchsafe unto Thy newly welcomed one Thy gifts and Thy bestowals, and the fruits of the tree of Thy grace!
>
> *Bahá'u'lláh*

For Consultation

Go through this prayer with your teacher. What is 'Thy Trust'? It sounds very loving. What does it mean to 'compass Thy dominions'? It sounds like it means both worlds. Is the newly welcomed one the person who has just died?

DAY 12

A Reading to Remember

O Son of Earth! Know, verily, the heart wherein the least remnant of envy yet lingers, shall never attain My everlasting dominion …

Activity

A lot of people place their security in things that won't last very long. They might think their homes, cars or possessions are the most important things in their life. Make a storyline. Start the story with a person getting lots of new possessions. Then show how other people see all this. Does the person have friends and lots of fun? Does he lose these things? Is he a happy person? Then suppose you end the storyline with a moral. Work on this with your teacher.

DAY 13

A Reading to Remember

O Son of Earth! Know, verily, the heart wherein the least remnant of envy yet lingers, shall never attain My everlasting dominion …

Activity

One of the remarkable traits of the Bahá'ís is their hospitality. When you go to the Feast or even to visit, you will receive love and honour from the Bahá'ís. Often there will be an abundance of food and warmth.

Draw a picture of your Feast. You can take it to the Nineteen Day Feast to show the friends.

For Consultation

What is the difference between sharing food and wanting to look after only your own needs? Is it valuable to share with each other what God gives us?

DAY 14

A Reading to Remember

O Son of Earth! Know, verily, the heart wherein the least remnant of envy yet lingers, shall never attain My everlasting dominion …

Activity

If you went fishing and caught so many fish that you couldn't use them all, you could throw some back in the water and share some with friends. This would not be greed. It would be sharing your good fortune with others. Write in your diary about sharing with others.

For Consultation

How do you stop being greedy?

DAY 15

A Reading to Remember

O Son of Earth! Know, verily, the heart wherein the least remnant of envy yet lingers, shall never attain My everlasting dominion, nor inhale the sweet savours of holiness …

Activity

We can't always share the good things we know with our friends but we should realize that they are in God's dominion and are a part of His plan for life. You are you and they are they and we are all God's children. We should all love each other and have pure thoughts in our dealings with one another. List some of the ways we should care for our friends.

For Consultation

We can't always teach the Faith to those who are not interested or who think we are wrong. But we can pray for all humankind. Discuss this.

DAY 16

A Reading to Remember

O Son of Earth! Know, verily, the heart wherein the least remnant of envy yet lingers, shall never attain My everlasting dominion, nor inhale the sweet savours of holiness …

Activity

Does your fund box get heavier all the time? Wonderful! When it gets very full, perhaps your parents can help you to contribute what you have saved to your national fund. With this giving, you ensure the continuation of the growth of our Faith and you can really feel a part of the projects which the Bahá'ís of the world are undertaking.

For Consultation

Who could be sad when the world is getting closer to the Day of God? As Bahá'ís work, the world changes! Discuss this.

DAY 17

A Reading to Remember

O Son of Earth! Know, verily, the heart wherein the least remnant of envy yet lingers, shall never attain My everlasting dominion, nor inhale the sweet savours of holiness breathing from My kingdom of sanctity.

Bahá'u'lláh

Activity

Draw a picture of what you would take with you if you were going exploring in a forest. Write about your travels.

For Reflection

Every minute of the day we make choices about how we spend our life. Does what we learn in these lessons have anything to do with making good choices?

DAY 18

A Reading to Remember

See if you can remember the whole Hidden Word you have been learning this month.

Activity

Can you bake a cake with your teacher or parent? If you can bake together and measure together and admire the cake together, you will share a wonderful experience. Try to do your best to make the cake delicious. And remember not to be greedy and eat it all yourselves! It is much more fun to share it with everyone!

When you have chosen the recipe, you will need to make a lot of little decisions. (What do you have to bake with, how long will it take to bake, what pan will you use, etc.)

For Consultation

Are you confident when you make decisions? How can you become confident in your judgements?

DAY 19

A Reading to Remember

No doubt by now you know the beautiful Hidden Word by heart. Say it once again.

Activity

Your cake was probably a big success! Soon it will be the Feast of Loftiness. Again you will have the treasured opportunity to receive (or give) Bahá'í hospitality. To prepare for the Feast, let's read a Hidden Word.

> O Son of Being! Thy Paradise is My love; thy heavenly home, reunion with Me. Enter therein and tarry not. This is that which hath been destined for thee in Our kingdom above and Our exalted dominion.
>
> *Bahá'u'lláh*

You could copy this beautiful reading and share it at the devotional part of the Feast.

For Reflection

What did you learn during the month of Dominion? Congratulations!

Ayyám-i-Há
(Intercalary Days)

DAY 1

A Reading to Remember

O Son of Spirit! My first Counsel is this: Possess a pure, kindly and radiant heart, that thine may be a sovereignty ancient, imperishable and everlasting.

Bahá'u'lláh

For Reflection

The Bahá'í Calendar

There are nine holy days in the Bahá'í calendar: Naw-Rúz; the Birth of the Báb; the Declaration of the Báb; the Martyrdom of the Báb; the Birth of Bahá'u'lláh; the first, ninth and twelfth Days of Riḍván; and the Ascension of Bahá'u'lláh. Bahá'ís do not work or go to school on these days. Two other days are celebrated in honour of 'Abdu'l-Bahá. These are also holy days but people can go to work or school. They are the Ascension of 'Abdu'l-Bahá and the Day of the Covenant.

Today we begin the Intercalary Days or Ayyám-i-Há. It is a happy celebration, which we will discuss tomorrow. For now, enjoy a special time with your family and friends. Happy Ayyám-i-Há!

A Reading to Remember

O Son of Spirit! My first Counsel is this . . .

Activity

The Bahá'í Calendar

Ayyám-i-Há is a period of four or five days (depending on whether it is 'leap' year) in which we take time especially to look after the poor or to care for the sick. We also make and give presents and show hospitality to our friends. In some countries there are children's parties and an atmosphere of fun and festivity prevails.

For Consultation

Would your family like to have a party for your friends? Would you like to visit and comfort the poor? Is there a home for the elderly you would like to visit? Happy Ayyám-i-Há!

DAY 3

A Reading to Remember

O Son of Spirit! My first Counsel is this: Possess a pure, kindly and radiant heart . . .

For Reflection

Bahá'í Calendar

The reason Bahá'u'lláh gave us the Intercalary Days (Ayyám-i-Há) is to balance the calendar. We celebrate Ayyám-i-Há between the 18th and 19th Bahá'í months. Because the Bahá'í calendar is a solar (sun) calendar, these days make it add up to a solar year! Happy Ayyám-i-Há!

DAY 4

A Reading to Remember

O Son of Spirit! My first Counsel is this: Possess a pure, kindly and radiant heart, that thine may be a sovereignty ancient, imperishable and everlasting.

Bahá'u'lláh

Activity

Bahá'í Calendar

The Bahá'í calendar replaces earlier calendars. It is one of the signs of a Manifestation of God that He establishes a calendar for His Revelation. The Bahá'í calendar provides all people with one unified calendar.

Have a look at your Bahá'í calendar. Notice the 19 months, each of which has 19 days. Look for the Intercalary Days and the holy days. Happy Ayyám-i- Há!

DAY 5

A Reading to Remember

O Son of Spirit! My first Counsel is this: Possess a pure, kindly and radiant heart, that thine may be a sovereignty ancient, imperishable and everlasting.

Bahá'u'lláh

For Consultation

Bahá'í Calendar

On the last day of Ayyám-i-Há the Bahá'ís think forward to the fast which will now begin. Two of the laws brought by Bahá'u'lláh provide for our constant growth and spiritual purification: these are the twin laws of fasting and obligatory prayer. Ask your teacher about the effect these two laws have on us individually and on the Bahá'í world as a whole. Happy Ayyám-i-Há!

19

Month of 'Alá' (Loftiness)

A Prayer to Remember

Welcome to the month of Loftiness, the final month of the Bahá'í year. During the month the adult Bahá'ís will fast and we will learn about the fast.

> O Thou kind Lord! Graciously bestow a pair of heavenly wings unto each of these fledglings, and give them spiritual power that they may wing their flight through this limitless space and may soar to the heights of the Abhá Kingdom.
>
> 'Abdu'l-Bahá

Activity

A fledgling is a baby bird. Do you see that 'Abdu'l-Bahá used that word in His prayer? Draw a beautiful baby bird winging her way through the skies.

For Consultation

Loftiness means 'of imposing height, towering or elevated in character, exalted and noble'. Is your bird flying in a lofty space?

A Prayer to Remember

Learn this prayer of 'Abdu'l-Bahá by heart. Practise it every day during the month of Loftiness.

> O Thou kind Lord! Graciously bestow a pair of heavenly wings unto each of these fledglings, and give them spiritual power that they may wing their flight through this limitless space and may soar to the heights of the Abhá Kingdom.
>
> 'Abdu'l-Bahá

Activity

The Bahá'í fast lasts for 19 days. Adult Bahá'ís from the age of 15 do not eat or drink from sunrise until sunset. They replace food and water with a lofty feeling and spiritual awareness! Special prayers are recited to ask God for purification and assistance.

When you eat, you eat material food. Try it. Go to the cupboard, choose something to eat (get permission) and sit down. Eat the food. You are fulfilling a need of your body.

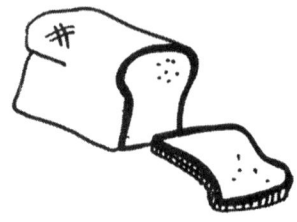

For Consultation

Why do our bodies need food?

A Prayer to Remember

O Thou kind Lord!

Activity

During the fast your parents may rise before sunrise and have breakfast. They will pray. It is a sacrifice for people to change their routines this way, even if the food is not missed. You might like to join them for these early prayers.

For Consultation

If you were older and fasting, what food would you miss the most?

A Prayer to Remember

O Thou kind Lord! Graciously bestow a pair of heavenly wings …

Activity

Learn more about the Bahá'í fast.

During the day, although your parents still go about their daily work and activities, they will not have anything to eat or drink during their breaks. They will pray. They may, at first, feel hunger pangs but they know they can do this for Bahá'u'lláh. They may get a bit irritable because of the upset to their usual pattern of eating but you can understand that!

For Consultation

What happens during the day when someone says to your parent, 'Where's your lunch?' How does your parent handle this? Why not ask?

A Prayer to Remember

O Thou kind Lord! Graciously bestow a pair of heavenly wings …

Activity

In the evening your parents will pray. They will prepare the dinner or an evening meal and wait for the sunset. Then suddenly, at the hour of sunset, they are able to eat again! It is really very exciting. They feel great because they have done as they were asked by Bahá'u'lláh. Be considerate of them as they break their fast and perhaps offer to wash the dishes after dinner.

For Consultation

What do you know about Bahá'í law? Is fasting a law?

A Prayer to Remember

O Thou kind Lord! Graciously bestow a pair of heavenly wings ...

Activity

There is another kind of food. Did you know that? It is spiritual food and it tastes better all the time! Spiritual food must look interesting. Why don't you draw a picture of a 'spiritual food dinner'?

For Consultation

Explain to your teacher what your dinner is all about. Would you like to eat this dinner?

A Prayer to Remember

O Thou kind Lord! Graciously bestow a pair of heavenly wings unto each of these fledglings ...

Activity

Long, long ago people fasted for many reasons. Some people fasted to receive guidance. People searching for the Báb, at the advent of His Revelation, often fasted for long periods of time and then set out to look for Him. Some of these spiritual people became Letters of the Living – a title give by the Báb to the first people who found Him.

Read this passage of 'Abdu'l-Bahá about this station:

> O ye apostles of Bahá'u'lláh. May my life be sacrificed for you! … Behold the portals which Bahá'u'lláh hath opened before you! Consider how exalted and lofty is the station you are destined to attain, how unique the favours with which you have been endowed.
>
> 'Abdu'l-Bahá

For Consultation

What is 'Abdu'l-Bahá saying to the Bahá'ís? Should we strive to serve Bahá'u'lláh?

A Prayer to Remember

> O Thou kind Lord! Graciously bestow a pair of heavenly wings unto each of these fledglings …

Activity

Once we receive guidance on a question we have, we should make our decision and make a practical effort to carry it out.

Do you ever have a problem for which you need guidance? The time of fasting is often a time to seek this guidance. The fast gives us help in many unseen ways. It is all part of the spiritual growth that we seek. Can you write a poem about growing up?

For Consultation

Show the poem to your parents. Do they understand it? Explain what you mean to them so they can share your feelings.

A Prayer to Remember

O Thou kind Lord! Graciously bestow a pair of heavenly wings unto each of these fledglings, and give them spiritual power ...

Activity

Even though your parents are fasting, they will still provide you with all the meals you need. This might be a good time to reflect on what it means to respect your parents. Just as God shelters us and provides us with our needs, so do parents nurture their children. The children even benefit from the effects of their parents' fast. As the parents abide by the will of God, the children are safe and secure.

Could you make a part of your parents' evening meal tonight? This will show them how you support them as they fast.

For Consultation

Why is our spirit so free? How does it soar up into the clouds while we live with our feet on the ground?

A Prayer to Remember

O Thou kind Lord! Graciously bestow a pair of heavenly wings unto each of these fledglings, and give them spiritual power ...

Activity

At the end of the fast comes the Bahá'í New Year. It is called Naw-Rúz and is a holy day. It is separate from the Nineteen Day Feast of Bahá. The Naw-Rúz

Feast should be held between sunset on 20 March and sunset on 21 March. It is a festive occasion when the friends gather to celebrate the end of the fast and the beginning of the new year.

What do you do at Naw-Rúz in your community? Ask your teacher to help you prepare something special for this Naw-Rúz.

Day 11

A Prayer to Remember

O Thou kind Lord! Graciously bestow a pair of heavenly wings unto each of these fledglings, and give them spiritual power that they may wing their flight …

Activity

Work on your Naw-Rúz project. It could be a decoration for the Feast table or gifts for the Bahá'ís or whatever you can manage.

For Consultation

All of the magnificence of the attributes of God which we have studied throughout the year come to mind now. The fast is also a time to feel grateful for the privilege of serving God as a Bahá'í. Discuss what it means to be grateful. What does it mean when we say that the Revelation of Bahá'u'lláh has taught us everything we need to know in this age.

A Prayer to Remember

O Thou kind Lord! Graciously bestow a pair of heavenly wings unto each of these fledglings, and give them spiritual power that they may wing their flight …

Activity

Work on your Naw-Rúz project again.

For Consultation

These words of 'Abdu'l-Bahá illustrate for us the lofty station our thoughts can achieve:

> If we suffer, it is the outcome of material things, and all the trials and troubles come from this world of illusion.
>
> For instance, a merchant may lose his trade and depression ensues. A workman is dismissed and starvation stares him in the face. A farmer has a bad harvest, anxiety fills his mind. A man builds a house which is burnt to the ground and he is straightway homeless, ruined, and in despair.
>
> All these examples are to show you that the trials which beset our every step, all our sorrow, pain, shame and grief, are born in the world of matter; whereas the spiritual Kingdom never causes sadness. A man living with his thoughts in this Kingdom knows perpetual joy. The ills all flesh is heir to do not pass him by, but they only touch the surface of his life, the depths are calm and serene.
>
> *'Abdu'l-Bahá*

Discuss this passage.

DAY 13

A Prayer to Remember

> O Thou kind Lord! Graciously bestow a pair of heavenly wings unto each of these fledglings, and give them spiritual power that they may wing their flight through this limitless space …

Activity

There is a strong connection between the body and the spirit. Read this passage of Bahá'u'lláh and picture it in your mind.

> O Lord! The tongue of my tongue and the heart of my heart and the spirit of my spirit and my outward and inmost beings bear witness to Thy unity and Thy oneness, Thy power and Thine omnipotence, Thy grandeur and Thy sovereignty, and attest Thy glory, loftiness and authority. I testify that Thou art God and that there is none other God besides Thee.
>
> *Bahá'u'lláh*

For Consultation

Bahá'u'lláh says His outward and inmost beings bear witness to God. This is a very lofty statement. Where do we find spirit? Is it in our body or a part of the connection between this world and the world of God?

DAY 14

A Prayer to Remember

> O Thou kind Lord! Graciously bestow a pair of heavenly wings unto each of these fledglings, and give them spiritual power that they may wing their flight through this limitless space …

Activity

You might like to work on your Naw-Rúz project again. If not, why don't you spend some time meditating on what we have been reading the past few days?

For Consultation

Our thoughts are a strong factor in how we live. If we think of God rather than ourselves, it helps us to be Bahá'ís. How do we do that?

DAY 15

A Prayer to Remember

O Thou kind Lord! Graciously bestow a pair of heavenly wings unto each of these fledglings, and give them spiritual power that they may wing their flight through this limitless space and may soar to the heights of the Abhá Kingdom.

'Abdu'l-Bahá

Activity

Do you have some music that you would like to listen to and sing along with? If you still have work to do on your project, you can enjoy doing both.

For Consultation

Think some thoughts that make you happy. Discuss with your teacher the kind of thoughts they are. What thoughts does your teacher prefer?

DAY 16

A Prayer to Remember

See if you can say the whole prayer by heart.

Activity

Write to your pen pal and wish him or her a happy Naw-Rúz! Send a photo of yourself if you have one and send one of the drawings you have done that might make a thoughtful gift.

No doubt you appreciate the friendship of your pen pal. Friends like to share their hopes and thoughts. Maybe you can arrange to see each other some time!

DAY 17

A Prayer to Remember

Say the whole prayer by heart, if you can.

Activity

Draw the sunrise. If you haven't really seen it, get your parents to describe it. Or you might like to wake up early to say dawn prayers with your parents and watch the sun come up.

For Consultation

Have you been up early in the morning with your parents as they begin their fast? What do you think of the peaceful sunrise time? It is a special time of the day when our thoughts rest on the beauty of nature.

A Prayer to Remember

Recite the prayer you have been learning.

Activity

One more day before the end of Loftiness! Write in your diary your thoughts about this month.

I hope you have memorized your prayer and can offer to say it at the Holy Day or the Nineteen Day Feast. Practise it one more time now.

For Consultation

What is loftiness? Is it possible to have lofty thoughts in daily life?

A Prayer to Remember

Recite your prayer one last time this month.

Activity

It's time to appreciate all the work you have done, learning, sharing and giving of yourself through this year. It's time to reflect on all the things you have learned together. To do this, you and your teacher or parent could do a skit about two people having a conversation about the 'old year'. Fantasize and imagine and pretend all you wish in your skit. Maybe you will perform it for your parents!

For Consultation

Your work doesn't end here. You will learn and grow forever.
I hope you will long remember these few minutes a day. Happy Naw-Rúz!

Bibliography

'Abdu'l-Bahá. *Paris Talks*. London: Bahá'í Publishing Trust, 1967.
— *The Promulgation of Universal Peace*. Wilmette, IL: Bahá'í Publishing Trust, 1982.
— *Selections from the Writings of 'Abdu'l-Bahá*. Haifa: Bahá'í World Centre, 1978.
— *Some Answered Questions*. Wilmette, IL: Bahá'í Publishing Trust, 1981.
— *Tablets of the Divine Plan*. Wilmette, IL: Bahá'í Publishing Trust, 1977.

Bahá'í Prayers: A Selection. London: Bahá'í Publishing Trust, 1967.

Bahá'í Prayers: A Selection of Prayers revealed by Bahá'u'lláh, the Báb and 'Abdu'l-Bahá. Wilmette, IL: Bahá'í Publishing Trust, 1991.

Bahá'í World Faith. Wilmette, IL: Bahá'í Publishing Trust, 2nd edn. 1976.

Bahá'u'lláh. *Gleanings from the Writings of Bahá'u'lláh*. Wilmette, IL: Bahá'í Publishing Trust, 1983.
— *The Hidden Words*. Wilmette, IL: Bahá'í Publishing Trust, 1990.
— *The Kitáb-i-Aqdas*. Haifa: Bahá'í World Centre, 1992.
— *Prayers and Meditations*. Wilmette, IL: Bahá'í Publishing Trust, 1987.
— *The Seven Valleys and the Four Valleys*. Wilmette, IL: Bahá'í Publishing Trust, 1991.
— *Tablets of Bahá'u'lláh*. Wilmette, IL: Bahá'í Publishing Trust, 1988.

Balyuzi, H. M. *Bahá'u'lláh, The Word Made Flesh*. Oxford: George Ronald, 1963.

Braun, Eunice and Chance, Hugh E. *A Crown of Beauty*. Oxford: George Ronald, 1982.

Compilation of Compilations, The. Prepared by the Universal House of Justice 1963–1990. 2 vols. [Sydney]: Bahá'í Publications Australia, 1991.

Faizi, Gloria. *Stories about 'Abdu'l-Bahá*. New Delhi: Bahá'í Publishing Trust, 1987.

Ford, R. E. *Bahá'í Principles for Children*. [London]: Bahá'í Publishing Trust, 1974.

Fozdar, Shirin. *Lord Buddha and Maitreya Amitabha*. New Delhi: Bahá'í Publishing Trust, no date.

Furútan, 'Alí-Akbar. *Mothers, Fathers and Children: Practical Advice to Parents*. Oxford; George Ronald, 1984.

Gail, Marzieh. *Bahá'í Glossary*. Wilmette, IL: Bahá'í Publishing Trust, 1976.

Gash, Andrew. *Stories from 'Star of the West'*, Mona Vale, N.S.W., Bahá'í Publications Australia, 1985.

Holy Bible. King James Version. London: Collins, 1839.

Keenness of Vision. Reference Materials for Auxiliary Board Members and Assistants, prepared by the Continental Board of Counsellors in Europe. 2nd edn. 1994.

Let Thy Breeze Refresh Them: Bahá'í Prayers and Tablets for Children. Oakham: Bahá'í Publishing Trust, 1976.

Magnified Be Thy Name: Prayers and Thoughts for Children from the Bahá'í Holy Writings. comp. Child Education Committee of the National Spiritual Assembly of the Bahá'ís of the United Kingdom. London: Bahá'í Publishing Trust, 1976.

Moffett, Ruth J. *New Keys to the Book of Revelation*. New Delhi: Bahá'í Publishing Trust, 2nd edn. 1980.

Morris, William, ed. *The Heritage Illustrated Dictionary of the English Language*. New York: McGraw-Hill, 1969.

The Mystery of God. comp. Iran F. Muhajer. London: Bahá'í Publishing Trust, 1979.

O God, Guide Me! Wilmette, IL: Bahá'í Publishing Trust, 1974.

O God, My God … Bahá'í Prayers and Tablets for Children and Youth. Wilmette, IL: Bahá'í Publishing Trust, 1984.

Phelps, Myron H. *The Master in 'Akká*. Los Angeles: Kalimát Press, 1985.

Quickeners of Mankind: Pioneering in a World Community. Wilmette, IL: Bahá'í Publishing Trust, 1998.

Root, Martha. 'Táhirih's Message to the Modern World', *Bahá'í World*, vol. 8, pp. 918–21.

Shoghi Effendi. *God Passes By*. Wilmette, IL: Bahá'í Publishing Trust, rev. edn. 1974.

— *The Promised Day is Come*. Wilmette, IL: Bahá'í Publishing Trust, rev. edn. 1980.

Star of the West. rpt. Oxford: George Ronald, 1984.

Taafaki, Irene. *Thoughts: Education for Peace and One World*. Oxford: George Ronald, 1986.

Taherzadeh, Adib. *The Revelation of Bahá'u'lláh, vol. 1*. Oxford: George Ronald, 1974.

Where the Prayers and Readings Come From

Month 1: Bahá
    Days 1–8, 10, 13: Bahá'u'lláh, in *Bahá'í Prayers* (US), p. 117.
    Day 6: Fozdar, *Lord Buddha and Maitreya Amitabha*, p. 11.
    Day 9: 'Abdu'l-Bahá, *Selections*, p. 254.

Month 2: Jalál
    Days 1–8, 19: Bahá'u'lláh, in *Bahá'í Prayers* (UK), p. 60.
    Day 2: Bahá'u'lláh, *Gleanings*, p. 250.
    Day 4: Bahá'u'lláh, *Gleanings*, p. 295.
    Day 11: Bahá'u'lláh, *Prayers and Meditation*, pp. 126–7.
    Day 16: 'Abdu'l-Bahá, *Promulgation of Universal Peace*, pp. 33–4.

Month 3: Jamál
    Day 1: *O God, My God, Bahá'í Prayers and Tablets for Children and Youth*, no. 30.
    Day 2: Phelps, *The Master in 'Akká*, pp. 4–10.
    Day 8: Bahá'u'lláh, *Gleanings*, p. 30.
    Day 14: Bahá'u'lláh, *Gleanings*, p. 7.
    Day 19: 'Abdu'l-Bahá, *Selections*, p. 35.

Month 4: 'Aẓamat
    Day 1: Bahá'u'lláh, *Hidden Words*, Arabic no. 65.
    Day 3: Braun and Chance, *Crown of Beauty*, p. 91.
    Day 6: Bahá'u'lláh, quoted in Shoghi Effendi, *Promised Day is Come*, p. 121.
    Day 10: Bahá'u'lláh, *Kitáb-i-Aqdas*, p. 21, para. 5.
    Day 13: *Bahá'í Prayers*, p. 28.

Month 5: Núr
    Days 1, 4–10, 12–14: *O God, My God*, no. 21.
    Day 5: Adapted from *Star of the West*, vol. 13, no. 7, p. 182 by Andrew Gash.
    Day 6: Adapted from *Star of the West*, vol. 13, no. 7, pp. 182–3 by Andrew Gash.
    Day 7: Adapted from *Star of the West*, vol. 13, no. 7, p. 183 by Andrew Gash.
    Day 8: Adapted from *Star of the West*, vol. 13, no. 7, p. 183 by Andrew Gash.
    Day 8: Bahá'u'lláh, *Hidden Words*, Persian no. 32.
    Day 9: Adapted from *Star of the West*, vol. 13, no. 7, pp. 183–4 by Andrew Gash.

Month 6: Raḥmat
    Days 1–3: The Báb, *Selections*, p. 193.
    Days 4–6: Bahá'u'lláh, Shoghi Effendi, *Advent of Divine Justice*, p. 78.
    Days 7–9: Bahá'u'lláh, in *Bahá'í Prayers*, p. 87.
    Days 10–12: 'Abdu'l-Bahá, in *Bahá'í Prayers*, p. 152.
    Days 13–15: 'Abdu'l-Bahá, in *Bahá'í Prayers*, p. 37.
    Days 16–19: 'Abdu'l-Bahá, in *Bahá'í Prayers*, p. 204.

Month 7: Kalimát
    Days 1, 3–16: Bahá'u'lláh, *Prayers and Meditations*, p. 233.
    Day 8: Bahá'u'lláh, *Tablets*, p. 156.
    Day 11: Balyuzi, *Bahá'u'lláh*, p. 39
    Day 13: Bahá'u'lláh, *Gleanings*, p. 96.
    Day 14: Bahá'u'lláh, *Hidden Words*, Persian no. 66.
    Day 15: Bahá'u'lláh, *Hidden Words*, Persian no. 33.
    Day 17: Bahá'u'lláh, *Gleanings*, p. 295.

Month 8: Kamál
    Days 1–13: 'Abdu'l-Bahá, *Promulgation of Universal Peace*, p. 93.
    Day 8: 'Abdu'l-Bahá, *Tablets of the Divine Plan*, p. 50.
    Day 15: Bahá'u'lláh, in Shoghi Effendi, *Advent of Divine Justice*, p. 80.
    Day 16: Bahá'u'lláh, *Gleanings*, p. 218.
    Day 17: 'Abdu'l-Bahá, *Promulgation of Universal Peace*, p. 93.
    Day 18: 'Abdu'l-Bahá, in *Bahá'í Prayers*, p. 152.
    Day 19: Bahá'u'lláh, *Hidden Words*, Arabic no. 4.

Month 9: Asmá'
Days 1–2, 4–10: The Báb, *Selections*, p. 177.
Day 9: Shoghi Effendi, *God Passes By*, p. 139.
Day 11: 'Abdu'l-Bahá, quoted in Shoghi Effendi, *Bahá'í Administration*, p. 195.

Month 10: 'Izzat
Day 1: 'Abdu'l-Bahá, in *Bahá'í Prayers*, p. 37.

Month 11: Mashíyyat
Days 1–14: Bahá'u'lláh, *Gleanings*, p. 5.

Month 12: 'Ilm
Days 1–9, 16: 'Abdu'l-Bahá, in *O God, My God*, no. 32.
Day 10–15: Bahá'u'lláh, *Hidden Words*, Arabic no. 2.

Month 13: Qudrat
Days 1–8, 18: Bahá'u'lláh, *Prayers and Meditations*, pp. 257–8.
Day 10–15: Bahá'u'lláh, *Gleanings*, p. 34.

Month 14: Qawl
Days 1–19: Bahá'u'lláh, *Hidden Words*, Persian no. 44.
Days 5–7: Martha Root, 'Ṭáhirih's Message to the Modern World', *Bahá'í World*, vol. 8, pp. 918–21.

Month 15: Masá'il
Days 1–13: Bahá'u'lláh, *Hidden Words*, Arabic no. 12.
Day 11: 'Abdu'l-Bahá, *Some Answered Questions*, p. 79.
Day 12: 'Abdu'l-Bahá, *Some Answered Questions*, p. 188.
Day 13: 'Abdu'l-Bahá, *Some Answered Questions*, p. 201.
Day 14: See 'Abdu'l-Bahá, *Some Answered Questions*, pp. 268–72.
Day 15: Laura Clifford Barney, Preface to 'Abdu'l-Bahá, *Some Answered Questions*, p. xvii.
Day 16: 'Abdu'l-Bahá, *Promulgation of Universal Peace*, p. 335.
Day 19: Letter of the International Teaching Centre to Continental Counsellors, 5 December 1988, in *Keenness of Vision*, p. 91.

Month 16: Sharaf
    Day 1–5: Bahá'u'lláh, in *Compilation*, vol. 1, p. 386.
    Day 7: Faizi, *Stories About 'Abdu'l-Bahá*, pp. 21–2.
    Day 8: 'Abdu'l-Bahá, *Paris Talks*, p. 53.
    Day 9–11: Bahá'u'lláh, in *Bahá'í Prayers* (UK), p. 61.
    Day 12: Bahá'u'lláh, *Hidden Words*, Persian no. 3.
    Day 18: Faizi, *Stories About 'Abdu'l-Bahá*, p. 3.

Month 17: Sulṭán
    Days 1–16: Bahá'u'lláh, in *Bahá'í Prayers*, p. 34; see Bahá'u'lláh, *Epistle to the Son of the Wolf*, pp. ii–iv.
    Day 3: Bahá'u'lláh, *Hidden Words*, Persian no. 37.
    Day 9: Bahá'u'lláh, *Gleanings*, p. 16.
    Day 10: Shoghi Effendi, *World Order of Bahá'u'lláh*, p. 16.
    Day 13: 'Abdu'l-Bahá, in *Compilation*, vol. 1, pp. 274–5.

Month 18: Mulk
    Days 1–6: Bahá'u'lláh, *Prayers and Meditations*, p. 315.
    Day 3: Matthew 6:9–13.
    Days 8–17: Bahá'u'lláh, *Hidden Words*, Persian no. 6.
    Day 11: Bahá'u'lláh, in *Bahá'í Prayers*, p. 44.
    Day 19: Bahá'u'lláh, *Hidden Words*, Arabic no. 6.

Ayyám-i-Há
    Days 1–5: Bahá'u'lláh, *Hidden Words*, Arabic no. 1.

Month 19: 'Alá
    Days 1–15: 'Abdu'l-Bahá, in *O God, My God*, no. 20.
    Day 7: 'Abdu'l-Bahá, *Tablets of the Divine Plan*, pp. 47–8.
    Day 12. 'Abdu'l-Bahá, *Paris Talks*, p. 110.
    Day 13: Bahá'u'lláh, *Tablets of Bahá'u'lláh*, p. 114.